LIFE ON THE
NARROW PATH

A *Mountain Biker's Guide* to *Spiritual Growth* in *Troubled Times*

LIFE ON THE
NARROW PATH

A Mountain Biker's Guide to Spiritual Growth in Troubled Times

CLARK R. BURBIDGE

Bonneville Books
Springville, Utah

This is not an official publication of The Church of Jesus Christ of Latter-day Saints. The opinions and views expressed herein belong solely to the author and do not necessarily represent the opinions or views of Cedar Fort, Inc. Permission for the use of sources, graphics, and photos is also solely the responsibility of the author.

ISBN 13: 978-1-59955-457-0

Published by Bonneville Books, an imprint of Cedar Fort, Inc., 2373 W. 700 S., Springville, UT 84663
Distributed by Cedar Fort, Inc., www.cedarfort.com

Cover design by Danie Romrell
Cover design © 2011 by Lyle Mortimer
Edited and typeset by Kimiko Christensen Hammari and Kelley Konzak

Printed in the United States of America

10 9 8 7 6 5 4 3 2 1

Printed on acid-free paper

To my sweetheart, Leah, and each one of my children.

Having you with me on the trail
has made all the difference.

CONTENTS

ACKNOWLEDGMENTS

How does a person begin to share his gratitude for the marathon that occurs between the first glimmer of thought to the finished and published work? While it is an impossible task to adequately address, I wish to recognize a few who have made a difference in this process. I must first thank Jeff Zornow; Dan Sellers; Jonathan Butler; my sons Travis, Howie, and Neil; and numerous others for inspiration, conversation, friendship, and occasional first aid along the countless single track rides we have taken together.

For general and specific guidance given openly to a relative novice, I am grateful to those along the path who extended an experienced hand, including Dave Detton, Alan Peterson, Dale Merrill, Allen and Dawna Rozsa, Ralph Mabey, Travis and Shaunna Burbidge, Chelsea and Robert Merkley, David Egbert, Val Christensen, Mel Reeves, Vaughn Cox, Dan and Diana Paxton, Clark Moffat, Dr. Kim Bertin, Henry D. Eyring, Todd and Karin Cook, Don and Lora Albrecht, Brent Argyle, Jane Merrill, Janius Merrill, Lee Groberg, David Ridges, Robert Garff, George and Michele Easter, and my friends at the Bountiful Bicycle shop.

Moving from the written manuscript to a published work is fraught with many more blind corners and hazards than I imagined. I needed to develop several new areas of knowledge to address this process intelligently. My thanks to Karen Christofferson and Heather Moore of BookWise Publishing for their early tutoring and editing advice and especially to my newfound friends at Cedar Fort, Inc., Jennifer Fielding, Heather Holm, Kelley Konzak, Emily Showgren, Lee Nelson, and Lyle Mortimer, for believing in the message of *Life on the Narrow Path* while patiently instructing the mountain biker himself along an unfamiliar trail. I would also like to express my gratitude to my extended family and friends who have willingly read and reread chapters and given encouragement and strength at times when even seemingly insignificant efforts meant so much.

I cannot adequately express my thanks and love for each one of my children who have brought such joy to my life. To those still at home who so often have wondered if Dad would ever finish his book and get off the computer. To my parents, now passed on, who encouraged my progress even if they were unable to follow until later in life; I say thank you for teaching me to never give up on my dreams. And to my sweetheart, Leah, who loves without condition, gives without expectation of return, prays without ceasing, and provided tipping point encouragement when *Life on the Narrow Path* seemed to be at a dead end. She has patiently understood during nights when the computer continued to glare and provided a comforting hand when the disappointments of life mounted. She exemplifies all the best traits of a "Good Guide."

Finally, I cannot move on without expressing heartfelt appreciation to my Heavenly Father and my Savior Jesus Christ, who, through the influence and ministration of the Spirit, have been there during the very darkest days to let me know I was never alone; who have guided my hand and research in producing this work; and to whom I owe all that I have and all that I am. Thank you.

PREFACE

The mountain biking experiences referenced in this book are from my many rides on the Mueller Park Trail in Bountiful, Utah, from 1992 to 2010 unless otherwise specifically referenced. The Mueller Park Trail is an approximately 3.5-mile single track from the trailhead, which is at about a 5,200-foot elevation, to Big Rock (also referred to as Elephant Rock), where there is a beautiful view and nowadays a bench, the result of some young man's eagle project.

A single track, for the uninitiated, is a narrow one-lane trail. By comparison, a double track is commonly a track made by a four-wheeled vehicle. The trail continues another approximately 3 miles to Rudy's Flats, the summit (elevation about 7,100 feet), where many turn around and return down the Mueller Park side. The trail rises approximately 1,900 feet, the majority of which, about 1,100 feet, is to Big Rock. A person can continue on approximately 3 more miles from Rudy's Flats down the North Canyon side and then, using surfaced roads, complete a 12-mile loop back to the Mueller Park trailhead.

The trail can be busy on a Saturday or holiday but never feels crowded and is never a dull ride. It allows bikers, joggers, hikers, and the occasional horse or motorcycle, but it is extremely narrow and does not comfortably accommodate the latter two. It is well maintained, although in the early spring you should expect to find a tree or two that has fallen over the trail during the winter. I have ridden this trail as many as eighty times per year in all conditions, from snow and ice in the early spring through one hundred–degree days in the summer and as late as early December. In fact, one particularly dry year, I was able to ride up to Big Rock every month of the year except January. While riding, you may come across anything from horse-sized moose, deer, elk, porcupines, birds (including bald eagles or turkey vultures), numerous forest mammals, snakes (including the occasional rattlesnake), cougars, and many animals of the human and canine variety. It produces an atmosphere where every ride is a new adventure.

These rides allow much time to think about life and its challenges. They also allow time to examine life's problems and find solutions. But mostly they allow you the opportunity to appreciate the beauty of God's creations while getting some pretty solid exercise. I hope you enjoy these insights and find them helpful. Certainly this work does not pretend to present all the principles whereby a person may grow closer to God and find true joy in this life. Like mountain biking itself, spiritual growth comes as a process with new insights revealed along the way. I pray that as you make them part of your life, you will realize others as well.*

---

* NOTE: In most cases I refer to "he" in place of "he or she" to simplify presentation, unless, of course, I am referring to a specific individual. In addition, all scriptural references are from the Authorized King James Version of the Holy Bible.

INTRODUCTION

This is not really a book about mountain biking, yet it is very much about mountain biking and life. During my hundreds of mountain rides, I have had time to think. Sometimes the thoughts are random. Other times, difficult issues at work or dilemmas in dealing with family matters are the subject. However, it is not uncommon that I take time to contemplate principles of eternity and faith. During such thoughtful moments, I have found, surprisingly, numerous parallels between negotiating the narrow mountain single track and life's very similar strait gate and narrow path (Matthew 7:13–14; Luke 13:24). These lessons, absorbed precept upon precept and line upon line (Isaiah 28:9–10, 13) over years of participation in life, are what I hope you will find freshly illustrated through the conduit of this book. Learn these principles well. They will keep you safe and allow you to more fully enjoy your ride on both paths. As with mountain biking, using one or two of these principles will help, but it is in the mastery and effective employment of all the principles in concert that will make your experience along the narrow path both satisfying and successful.

In 1992, at the age of thirty-seven, I was diagnosed with degenerative arthritis in both my hips. It was a shock for someone who had been a two-sport athlete in high school and college and continued to live a very active life. Was the cause genetic, or was it some untreated injury that caused reduced blood flow to the joints? Was it a 1950s-era treatment for pigeon toes that produced misalignment of my hips, or moving three times in a year and two of those times carrying most of the items myself? Or was it just an unfortunate twist of fate?

Eighteen years later, no one has been able to determine the cause. It has been discouraging not to know, but in life we often don't get the easy *why* answers. In fact, life tends not to slow down for such moments; the steep climbs seem to come without regard for our need to catch our breath. On the other hand, we must recognize and efficiently utilize the easier stretches whenever they occur. This allows us to build momentum and reserve our strength for the tough climbs that surely will continue to loom before us—perhaps just around the next bend.

It has gradually dawned on me that discovering the reasons we face individual challenges doesn't matter very much. What does matter is accepting responsibility for where we are and how we manage the obstacles we come upon. God has a plan for us to return to His presence. It seems that our individual plan includes some personally tailored challenges that can be daunting. Yet, such individual trials, if faced with courage and faith, build and then strengthen the foundation of our spiritual growth and our ability to endure greater challenges as we continue to press forward. This is what John the Revelator referred to as "overcoming" (Revelation 2:7, 11, 17, 26; 3:5, 12, 21). At the very heart of the Lord's counsel, given through Isaiah, is that we receive "precept upon precept . . . line upon line; here a little, and there a little" (Isaiah 28:10), that we might be properly instructed as we are able to appreciate it. Notice that this growth occurs little by little based on our willingness to hear, learn, and do His will (Isaiah 28:14; Mark 4:24; Luke 6:49; James 1:22). Setbacks can and do provide, as we make correct choices and learn to "overcome," critical wisdom and the perspective necessary to drive our roots deep in good ground. This, combined with an attitude of ongoing nourishment through consistent and faithful "doing" (ibid.), allows the earth in which we are planted to become rich, secure, and productive. The blessing to those who diligently persevere, as the Savior stated, is that the resulting faith produces good fruit

(Matthew 7:16–20). In fact, the Savior went on to point out that it is the resulting "good treasure of the heart" that brings forth these good fruits (Matthew 12:35).

After my diagnosis, I was advised that I could continue with my high impact activities—soccer, running, basketball, softball, and skiing/jumping—or I could find new, lower impact pastimes like biking and swimming. If I chose poorly, I could expect one or two hip replacements and possibly life in a wheelchair. Of course the technology and prognosis for hip replacements has changed during the past eighteen years, but at the time the downside was sobering. If I chose wisely, the doctor explained, any operation could be put off for years, depending on how I felt. He didn't make any promises, but he did offer hope. Paul knew well the great power of hope grounded in faith: "The God of hope fill you with all joy and peace in believing, that ye may abound in hope, through the power of the Holy Ghost" (Romans 15:13) and "he that ploweth should plow in hope; and that he that thresheth in hope should be partaker of his hope" (1 Corinthians 9:10). To the Hebrews, Paul referred to hope as "an anchor of the soul" (Hebrews 6:19).

As you might expect, I did my best to use this anchor of my soul and choose wisely. I took up mountain biking and was fortunate to live at the mouth of a canyon with one of the state's greatest mountain bike trails. Because of the ideal location, I also discovered many who already enjoyed the activity and were glad to show me the ropes. Some would become lifelong friends and riding buddies. I also did other things like take supplements to build up my hips, keep my weight down, and emphasize activities that have been rigorous but lower impact. While I have not been the perfect example of diet or weight management and sometimes have participated in high impact activities, the results of these adjustments have been satisfying.

Eighteen years later, my joints feel better than they have since my midthirties, and as an added bonus, I have learned some important lessons about spiritual growth and finding happiness along the way in spite of continuing challenges. I have chosen my experiences with mountain biking as the context in which to frame these soul-saving lessons. Such principles have been an important part of my ability to continue to "stand" (1 Corinthians 16:13; Revelation 6:17) while enduring physical, family, financial, and spiritual challenges. Because of them, I am here, still standing, perhaps having lost some range of motion and flexibility but still active, happy, and spiritually progressing.

I am thankful to my Heavenly Father for always being there, for never pulling down the signposts, for placing wonderful individuals in my path at critical moments to strengthen me, and for allowing me to feel His love. I am grateful for my Savior Jesus Christ, who took upon Him all our sins and pains so we can overcome the difficulties of this life and return to live with our Father. I believe our part is to do our best and make the Savior's atoning sacrifice effective in our own lives through repentance, forgiveness of others, and excluding from our hearts all those things that canker and destroy, while replacing them with those things that are lovely and of good report (Philippians 4:8).

During the past eighteen years, these principles have strengthened me through illness, the passing of both my parents, personal and national economic crisis, wars, rumors of wars and terrorism, life's storms, challenges in my children's lives, family difficulties and all their attendant burdens, and the many other stressful and discouraging experiences of which life seems to be so full.

Today I continue to literally stand straight and tall. I still have my own hips and enjoy life more than ever. These gifts, along with my beautiful wife and our blended family of ten children, are an example of Heavenly Father returning twice our blessings as we continue faithful (Job 42:10). Looking back, I can see more clearly that overcoming much of the personal mountain range in which my climbs have taken place was only possible because I was carried in my Savior's loving arms, for it surely was a far greater challenge than I was capable of surmounting alone.

In my midthirties, I thought I understood the Atonement pretty well. What I didn't perceive was that real understanding only begins with studying the writings of prophets and apostles. It then increases with the fervent prayer that only life's trials can bring, especially those that require patience and long-suffering to endure and overcome on God's time frame. As we grow, the words of Isaiah regarding the mission and purpose of the Savior have new meaning: "Surely he hath borne our griefs, and carried our sorrows: yet we did esteem him stricken, smitten of God, and afflicted. But he was wounded for our transgressions, he was bruised for our iniquities: the chastisement of our peace was upon him; and with his stripes we are healed" (Isaiah 53:4–5). The Savior took upon Himself so much more than just our sins.

A common misunderstanding in reviewing Paul's writings to the Corinthians (1 Corinthians 10:13) is that God will not tempt or place any burden upon us that is greater than we can bear. In fact, a more complete understanding of the scripture reinforces that God will "make a way to escape, that ye may be able to bear it" (ibid.). Numerous other references support the idea that this life and the tests we face are specifically designed to be more than we can bear alone. That is the key. We cannot bear these by ourselves, but we can bear all things if we look to our Father and our Savior and bear it together. The Lord can give us rest (Matthew 11:28), make our burdens lighter (Matthew 11:30), or, through others, share the bearing of burdens (Galatians 6:2). Blindly attempting to forge on by ourselves, relying on our own strength, results in our body and soul eventually being crushed by the multiplying weight (Job 11:20; Psalm 38:4; Proverbs 11:5; Jeremiah 30:23).

While the details are personal, I do not believe I exaggerate much when I say that I understand some portion of what it is like to live through the first chapter of Job (Job 1:13–22; 2:1–10). But happily, I have also had the pleasure to learn what the last chapter of Job (Job 42:12–15) feels like. I prefer the last chapter without question. Could I have appreciated the blessings and understood with my heart had I not experienced the earlier chapters as well? I think not. And that has made the difference.

CHAPTER 1

Dwelling on Obstacles

Mountain biking requires a combination of conditioning, judgment, momentum, and balance. Biking on a narrow single track that often has steep drop-offs just inches off the track tests all of these abilities. This particular narrow track ride is often made more technical by loose or fixed rocks and roots, a number of narrow bridges, and logs placed cross-trail to prevent erosion. Dealing with these obstacles—along with hikers, joggers, and riders going both ways—requires continuous vigilance.

The first true principle of mountain biking is not to dwell on the obstacles. If you become focused on something on the trail—whether moving or stationary, loose or fixed— most likely your front tire will be drawn directly into it. This means you hit what you stare at. The experience can be particularly memorable if you are fixated on the drop-off on the edge of the trail or a biker moving in the opposite direction. This is not pleasant. Once I was following a rider down two switchbacks near the bottom of the trail. On the inside of both of these steep downhill turns are sturdy trees. She focused so hard on the inside of the switchbacks in an effort to avoid the trail's edge as she attempted the downhill turn that she crashed, impacting solidly, into the tree trunks on both bends. Both times she went over the handlebars and into the tree. Following the first crash, I stopped to give assistance and advice about this principle, but after the second one, she merely gave me an embarrassed look and waved me past. I had to agree—that is not something you see every day.

The result is often the same whether you have a lot of momentum or very little—you get to experience flying. Usually the flight is a short one over the front of your handlebars and onto your helmet or upper back. But it does look spectacular, and all mountain bikers eventually experience this. Such an experience usually does not result in permanent damage if you have the proper safety equipment. Spending a few moments on your back mentally checking through all your body parts to make sure you are still in one piece is a good idea before you try to pop back up again. Perhaps a little first aid to stop some bleeding, a quick check to make sure your bike isn't damaged, and you're ready to go, hopefully a bit wiser.

The life principle here is that it is often easier to focus on the negative. We look in the mirror and see our weaknesses and shortcomings. We seem to obsess that we are too much of one thing or not enough of something else. We are too tall or short, our weight is not right, or we don't like our hair. Our clothes are not in style or our body is not proportioned correctly. Our job isn't right or those we care about don't respond as we think they should. There are endless ways we tear ourselves down. Just as in mountain biking, if we dwell on these negative aspects, we will become them.

What do I mean? C. S. Lewis put it rather succinctly in the tenth of his fictional *Screwtape Letters*,[1] written from a senior devil to his apprentice nephew on how to handle their human subjects. He stated, "All mortals tend to turn into the thing they are pretending to be."[2] Simply, it is that we become comfortable with this kind of negative conversation, and others notice that we seem to be constantly unpleasant, tearing ourselves or others down or just dwelling on ourselves and creating a victim myth in our minds. Left unchecked, this can develop into an ever accelerating downward spiral of self-esteem. Unfortunately, those who dwell on the negative do not stop with themselves; they frequently turn to tearing down others. Some I have known who have fallen into this pattern cannot seem to carry on a conversation without including someone else's embarrassing failure or weakness.

No one really wants to be around such negative conversation. It pushes others away and then, of course, adds to the individual's downward, self-indulgent spiral. One serious trap associated with this self-victimization is to produce an atmosphere of helplessness in which no responsibility is taken. Everything is someone else's fault, we tell ourselves, or is caused by circumstances or unfairness out of our control. The subject of each conversation becomes lost in the trapped individual's growing obsession to prove there is nothing wrong with them and it is not their fault. This is discussed at length in chapter 7.

Those caught in such a trap continue reenforcing the same behavior, expecting things to change, and are unable to appreciate that they have the power to change their behavior and produce a different outcome. I remember counseling a young man on this subject a few years ago. I explained to him that he was like a person sitting in a car with a blown transmission. Things weren't working out when he pushed the gas, so his solution was to push ever harder on the gas and refuse any help from the mechanic. As a result, he wasted gas and got nowhere. Pursuing the same detrimental behavior more aggressively only uses up more energy without producing a positive result. Unfortunately, this course leads to frustration, anger, and bitterness, which in turn lead to hate and finally personal destruction as described more completely in chapter 6. This is a wide and well-worn path. Taking responsibility for your own acts or your role in a particular outcome regardless of how embarrassing or stressful it might be, is empowering. This is a basic step in both repentance and overcoming.

There is another way. The Apostle Paul counseled the Corinthians about seeing through a glass darkly (1 Corinthians 13:9–12). We learn from his letter that we must see ourselves as God sees us and put away childish things. He tells us that drawing closer to the Savior and seeking to see life as it really is, using revelation and truth, will allow us to grow from seeing in part to seeing perfectly (ibid.). One day we will see our Heavenly Father face to face and know ourselves as He knows us. Paul further tells us that we may proceed from glory to glory, thus gaining ever greater insight and understanding until we see as we are seen and receive a fulness of God's glory in His kingdom (2 Corinthians 3:18).

Pursuing this path then allows us to stand in front of that same mirror and learn to see ourselves as God sees us. He sees beyond our frailties and weaknesses; we can too. When the Lord told Samuel the prophet to go to the house of Jesse because He had prepared the next King of Israel from among Jesse's sons, Samuel obeyed. Jesse called each son before Samuel. The great prophet initially assumed that the next king would be the eldest son, Eliab, because he looked the part. The Lord's answer was instructive for Samuel as well as for us. In explaining that it was to be the youngest son, David, the Lord said, "Look not on his countenance, or on the height of his stature . . . for the Lord seeth not as man seeth; for man looketh on the outward appearance, but the Lord looketh on the heart" (1 Samuel 16:7).

David was brought in from the fields, and though he did not look the part, Samuel knew he was to be the next king and anointed him, "and the Spirit of the Lord came upon David from that day forward" (v. 13).

We are God's children, loved beyond measure. He is always there for us and has created this existence to allow us to become like Him and return to Him. By practicing this idea we begin to understand what He sees when He looks at us, and we can dwell on the positive. There is another interesting side effect of this kind of thinking. As we think of ourselves differently, we also begin to see others differently. We begin to see others as God sees them and feel charity more easily, which Paul, when counseling the Corinthians on spiritual gifts and desirable Christian qualities, refers to as the "greatest of these" (1 Corinthians 13:13).

You cannot avoid the obstacles you are dwelling on. They become part of you. Dwell on things that, as they become part of you, will lift you up, empower you, and make you a better person. It will draw others to you who sense that spirit of charity you carry. Be the kind of person who will make anyone who crosses your path grateful for having done so.

NOTES

1. C.S. Lewis, *The Screwtape Letters* (New York: HarperCollins, 2001), 50.
2. Ibid.

CHAPTER 2

Focusing Ahead

To access the Mueller Park Trail, you must cross a bridge from the parking lot. (There are six more bridges between this spot and Big Rock.) The bridge has three two-by-six boards running the length of it for strength and a six-inch drop-off at the end. Staying on one of these boards and executing a small hop at the end is helpful in avoiding your first little surprise of the trip. This skill comes into play later as you attempt to avoid obstacles and stay on the narrow track or one of the narrow bridges. The trick to riding in a relatively narrow straight line is not to look down at the line itself or even at the front of your tire. I don't know the physics or physiology of it, but focusing too closely on the front of your bike dramatically affects your balance. I believe it diminishes your brain's perspective of the environment and therefore results in an inability to balance and maintain a straight course.

Experience has taught me on many different trails that keeping the center of my focus about fifteen to twenty feet beyond my front tire and using my peripheral vision to pick up the closer-in details as well as the farther out details works best. Of course, a biker never stares at one spot; he is always shifting his field of vision, looking around quickly, and maintaining awareness. But the center of that range of movement and view always comes back to the location mentioned.

This focus allows you to anticipate and correct. It allows you to avoid problems and adjust gears as necessary. It creates perspective and balance. All these benefits mean that you can maintain momentum without unnecessary mishap.

In life, focusing ahead allows you many of the same advantages. We humans tend to act without thinking of the consequences, or if we recognize the possibility of a negative result, we are quick to discount it as being unlikely to happen to us. This near-term view of life is often referred to as a desire for immediate gratification or simply being shortsighted. This view opens us up to the influence of Satan. It is usually not the big compromises we make in life that steer us away from our eternal goals; it is a series of small deviations that pull us ever further off course. Virtually all selfish activity, bitterness, hate, indulgence, immorality, and other acts consist of a series of small errors. When observed by themselves, they may seem benign. However, when seen as a connected process, it is clear where they lead.

In *The Screwtape Letters*, the senior, more experienced devil, Screwtape, gives counsel to his young nephew, Wormwood, an apprentice devil, on how to effectively do his job with his specific human "patient." He says in his twelfth letter:

> You will say that these are very small sins; and doubtless, like all young tempters, you are anxious to be able to report spectacular wickedness. But do remember, . . . it does not matter how small the sins are provided that their cumulative effect is to edge the man away

from the Light and out into the Nothing. . . . Indeed
the safest road to Hell is the gradual one—the gentle
slope, soft underfoot, without sudden turnings, without
milestones, without signposts.[1]

This illustrates a second important principle. Anyone
who begins to fall under the influence of the adversary or
his minions will gradually be robbed of the joy and satisfaction of accomplishing anything worthwhile. All the
good and uplifting aspects of his life will steadily drain
away and be replaced by "nothing." Examples include loss
of warm relations with friends, good health, desire to serve
and grow, interest in a spiritually and physically healthy
lifestyle, enjoyment of wholesome and uplifting activities,
and the satisfaction and positive reinforcement that comes
with achievement. The adversary also robs him of the peace
that comes with a clear conscience and a life free from the
constant and ever-increasing burden of guilt, addiction, or
obsession. He loses motivation to strive, to achieve, to do
his best, and even the ability to care. Screwtape states in the
same letter, "He [the human] must not be allowed to suspect
that he is now, however slowly, heading right away from the
sun on a line which will carry him into the cold and dark of
utmost space."[2]

The adversary does not need to convince us to take one
fatal step. He accomplishes the same with distraction from
that which is good, leading to a lessening of our interest in
positive pursuits and then taking from us all the things that
are "something" in our lives and replacing them with "nothing." This could include obsessions on computer gaming,
music, or various other media that isolate us from others;
addicting substances or behaviors; or obsessions with things
instead of those who love us. Such things do no more than
pointlessly fill time. "Nothing" can also include replacement
of our positive human associations with counterfeit friendships with those who use us to justify their own insecurities

or acts. As stated in Screwtape's ninth letter, the goal is to give us "an ever increasing craving for an ever diminishing pleasure."[3] Why do so many slide into such an abyss? Satan knows that once he has taken from us everything we once valued and cherished, that lifted us up and made us feel joy, and has replaced it with "nothing," we will accept "anything" he offers because it is "something."

This also works the other way. It is the small good things we do, the slight corrections as we focus ahead, that make all the difference. The scriptures are replete with examples and counsel encouraging us to appreciate the power of small positive acts. We will discuss this idea at more length in chapter 3.

As we focus ahead, we keep life in perspective, and we are then able to more easily recognize, anticipate, and avoid the difficulties that cause problems along the trail. Our life continues to be something of value, and we consistently build upon the positive choices and acts that bring strength, purpose, and happiness. Now that is a trail that leads us somewhere worth going.

NOTES

1. C.S. Lewis, *The Screwtape Letters* (New York: HarperCollins, 2001), 60–61.
2. Ibid., 57.
3. Ibid., 44.

CHAPTER 3

Preparation and Anticipation

Preparation

If you take certain precautions before and during your ride, the experience will be much more safe and enjoyable. Such precautions include wearing a proper helmet, gloves, and safety glasses the entire time. I often see riders going uphill with their helmets unclipped, tied to their backpacks, or even absent. I can't help but wonder what they were thinking. Although you won't encounter danger each time you ride, you never know when your helmet or safety gear may save your life.

There is a spot on the trail about halfway to Big Rock, just before arriving at the "pipeline" (The underground Kern River Pipeline crosses the trail at this location, and you can see where the foliage was cut away twenty years ago to bury the pipe), where I once took a pretty good spill. It is a steep rock field of about 100 to 200 feet. I got out of my anticipated line and, because momentum is limited going uphill, when my front tire fell into a cradle with a solid rock at the end, it stuck perfectly. My body, of course, continued, without the bike, over the handlebars and onto my helmet and back. I sustained a pretty good cut on my leg and a couple of spectacular bruises from landing on the protruding rocks, but nothing permanent. How different the story might have been had I left my helmet home or clipped it to my backpack.

It is also common in the spring or fall to have branches hanging out on the trail. They may catch in your spokes, hit you in the glasses or helmet, and so forth. It is not always possible to see them coming. One downward ride about a half mile from the trailhead, my helmet struck a broken limb that was solid and did not give. It dazed me, and while I remained on my bike, I covered about 20 feet before I regained my senses. I have often wondered what might have happened without my helmet. Proper safety equipment can mean the difference between a brief interruption in your ride and a permanent interruption or change in your life. It is not worth the risk because you may be hot, you may feel inconvenienced, or "That is just the way you are."

The other preparation principle is embodied in the motto I use with my riding buddies: "You condition for the ride up, but you dress for the ride down." The first part of this is obvious; the ride will always be more enjoyable if you are in shape. The second part of the motto is unique to riding in the high mountains. One of the big mistakes made by mountain riders is that they dress too lightly. This is usually not a factor when riding uphill because of the heat your body generates, particularly your legs. However, when coming down, you are already wet with sweat, and on a cooler afternoon it can become quite cold, particularly on the inside, shaded parts of the trail. The wisdom is in making sure you layer so you have something extra to wear on the way down. In the early spring and late fall, this is an even bigger factor since the windchill temperatures going down can differ dramatically. This means carrying long-fingered gloves at certain times of the year is a must.

The other factor is weather, which in the mountains can change with little notice. I remember one ride with one of my most frequent riding buddies, Jeff, in mid-June. We got about twenty-five minutes into our ride and were in the last mile before arriving at Big Rock. The temperature was about fifty degrees, and the day was mostly clear and calm. Then, without warning, dark clouds appeared from directly over the mountain ridge to the north. Within ten minutes the temperature had dropped to near freezing, and we were in a snow blizzard with gusts of wind up to 40-plus mph.

As the wind picked up and the dark clouds streamed over the northern ridge, we immediately turned around, and before we had traveled 100 yards, snow was accumulating on the trail. Trees were being blown down, which we had to climb over with our bikes on our shoulders, and the metal and plastic brakes on our bikes became ice cold, making any firm grip increasingly difficult. I happened to have long-fingered gloves, which helped, but Jeff did not, and with about a half mile to go, his hands were in such bad shape he could no longer grip his brakes or handlebars. We dismounted and took a shortcut through undergrowth straight down the side of the mountain to what we knew was a picnic area that ran along the bottom of the canyon next to the stream. After jumping a 6-foot fence carrying our bikes and crossing a bridge (which had been damaged by a pine tree with a diameter of at least 2 feet that had been blown down on it), we were able to reach the parking lot and find warmth in one of the cars. It was a close one. While hypothermia was stalking us, frostbite and further tragedy were avoided because we turned around immediately and had layered for the cooler ride down.

Anticipation

I will use this term to describe advance adjustment to changing terrain while riding. The principle is to recognize a change in slope, let's say a climb, and make the speed and gear adjustments before you hit the upward slope. This allows momentum and a smooth gear transition to already be in place before they're needed. Maintaining momentum makes the climb easier while the early gear shift allows you to avoid the gears shifting during the climb or the chain jumping or slipping while on the hill. A chain that jumps or shifts while you are exerting maximum effort on a climb can cause unexpected pedal slippage, often resulting in a crash or injury. Early shifting before the pressure mounts allows the chain to adjust smoothly without any jerks or slippage.

These principles, applied to life, are much the same. When we are in difficulty, under stress, or amid great challenge, it is too late to prepare or effectively adjust. While it may be possible for some, it is at best much more difficult. We then are forced to endure with what we've got and hope that is enough. Sometimes others are involved who have wisely prepared both for themselves and for us. They may be able to ease the burden, but that is not always the case.

Early in World War II, the people of Narvik, Norway, learned this principle the hard way. In the far reaches of northern Norway, Narvik would seem to have been of little interest to the warring powers. However, Narvik was also the deep-sea port nearest to large deposits of iron ore much sought after by the Nazi regime for wartime production. Thus it was an early target for expansion. After a sharp but brief campaign, the allies were expelled from Norway and the Norwegian Army disbanded, leaving the Norwegian people at the mercy of the Third Reich. The sentiments expressed by the mayor of Narvik, Theodor Broch, provide profound insight. He recalled: "It was a harsh land we had, but never had it been so delightful, so desirable as now. Our leading men had already been driven abroad. Our ships had sunk or sailed away. All along the border [with Sweden] were young men like myself. Thousands more would follow. We had to leave to learn the one craft we had neglected. We had built good homes in the mountains, but we had neglected to fence them properly."[1]

Too often we convince ourselves that we have done enough, that our families are secure and our children safe from the terrible influences that we see devastating other families. We grow complacent and neglect the regular protective behavior that is so critical to our family's spiritual well-being. It is during such careless moments—when we have discarded, misplaced, or simply not kept in proper condition the protective armor given to us by God (Ephesians 6:10–18)—that Satan moves against us and we are faced with the trial of our lives. Our excuses that spiritual preparation was inconvenient or demanding then ring hollow.

So what are the steps we must take to prepare properly and anticipate the needs in advance of life's trials? First, we must develop a pattern of acting in advance of the need and not allowing circumstances to catch up with us and dictate our actions. This allows us to maintain meaningful freedom of choice. By not taking advantage of moments when we have the time to choose from a wide array of alternatives and by waiting until our options are down to one or two choices, we allow circumstances or others to dictate our actions. Doors of opportunity may close, which can leave us in crisis mode. Thus, delaying or abdicating a decision is also a choice. This particular kind of choice can severely limit our freedom to act.

Real preparation for spiritual challenges is found in one of the Savior's best known parables. It is repeated in three of the four gospels, although I will refer here to the gospel of Mark. It provides insight into the four states of man on this earth with respect to receiving the word of God. It also provides key understanding of what makes the difference between success and failure in spiritual growth.

Mark first tells us that some seeds fell by the wayside but were devoured by involvement with sin and direct control of the adversary (Mark 4:4, 14–15). Some will make choices that place them on his turf, where meaningful freedom to act does not exist.

Another group of seeds, he tells us, fell among thorns and began to grow but were choked by distraction and absorption with the cares of the world (Mark 4:7, 18–19). These individuals chose to abdicate their freedom to choose.

A further group of seeds fell on stony ground and were unable to gain sufficient root, so when the sun (the trials of the world) came, they were scorched, withered, and died (Mark 4:5–6, 16–17). Their intent was good and they were good people, but they failed to prepare adequately, so they were not strong enough to overcome. The first positive clue of how to do it right is given here when the writer tells us that the roots had "no depth of earth" (Mark 4:5).

The last group of seeds fell on good ground, we are told, and were nourished and grew (Mark 4:8, 20).

It is clear that we need to cultivate "good ground"—what is also called "deepness of earth"—to enable us to develop deep roots. This allows us to withstand and overcome the difficult times that come as part of life on this earth. How, then, do we develop this deepness of earth that allows us to be properly prepared and anticipate such times? In the Sermon on the Mount, the Savior tells us that as we "hunger and thirst after righteousness" we will be filled (Matthew 5:6). This regular nourishment that results from our efforts will, if applied with great care, get root and bring forth the fruit of everlasting life. He also warns us where there is no nourishment and care, there cannot be fruit (Matthew 7:16–20). He further counsels us that we must be patient and diligent and have our eyes looking forward to the successful result that we may become the "children of your Father which is in heaven" (Matthew 5:45).

Nourishment does not happen all at once. A person cannot pour the water needed for an entire growing season on the seeds the first day. Nor can he expect the seed to grow if the ground is not prepared, tilled, and nourished. Nourishing takes time and occurs little by little. It must be consistently applied over long periods of our lives. We have been given daily, weekly, and monthly resources that we must take advantage of to provide the regular requirement of spiritual nutrients that is necessary to develop deepness of earth. As we develop good habits such as regularly holding personal and family prayer, personal and family scripture study, and family activity nights; observing family meals together; attending church, synagogue, and temple services regularly; cultivating morality, honesty, and service; and developing a heart that is willing to follow the Lord's inspiration wherever it leads, we prepare ourselves for the great trials that are necessary for us to become who we must be. We also obtain the Spirit for our guide so that when we approach difficulties we can adjust our gears, maintain momentum, and come through the storms we face. We are not promised that this process won't leave us bruised and battered, but we will not wither and die because we remain faithfully and deeply rooted in good ground. It is not usually the great one-time sacrifices that help us become who we must be to return to our Heavenly Father; rather it is the consistent and faithful application of small things that makes the difference. The scriptures are replete with such examples and counsel, for God knows we must learn this important principle.

James reminds us, "Behold, we put bits in the horses' mouths, that they may obey us; and we turn about their whole body. Behold also the ships, which though they be so great, and are driven of fierce winds, yet are they turned about with a very small helm, whithersoever the governor listeth" (James 3:3–4).

The Savior taught of the power of even a small amount of faith: "For verily I say unto you, If ye have faith as a grain of mustard seed, ye shall say unto this mountain, Remove hence to yonder place; and it shall remove; and nothing shall be impossible unto you" (Matthew 17:20).

Goliath was defeated and Israel saved by a small smooth stone slung by a lad (1 Samuel 17:40).

When Naaman came to Elisha to be healed of leprosy, he was given what seemed to be a simple task in order to be healed. Naaman was reluctant, thinking its performance was beneath the captain of the host of the king of Syria, but was convinced by the argument of his servants to proceed and was healed. "And his servants came near, and spake unto him, and said, . . . if the prophet had bid thee do some great thing, wouldest thou not have done it? how much rather then, when he saith to thee, Wash, and be clean? Then went he down, and dipped himself seven times in Jordan, according to the saying of the man of God: and his flesh came again like unto the flesh of a little child, and he was clean" (2 Kings 5:13–14).

The children of Israel were healed by a simple act of obedience: looking to the brazen serpent Moses was commanded to raise up (Numbers 21:4–9).

After fishing through the night and catching nothing, Simon Peter and his companions were commanded to make a small change in their approach by casting their nets over the right side of the boat. This small act of obedience produced a miraculous result: The "multitude of fishes" was so great that they were unable to pull it into the boat (John 21:5–6).

Yes, we know these stories and teachings, but do we really believe as David when he told Goliath, "this day will the Lord deliver thee into mine hand . . . that all the earth may know that there is a God in Israel" (1 Samuel 17:46)? God sent us here to achieve greatness, but great results are accomplished by consistently doing small things. Know that there is a God in the world today and nothing is impossible for Him. It takes faith and inspiration to prepare for winter on a sunny day. It takes deep roots in good ground during winter storms to know that spring will return. It takes time every day to build and organize a righteous life and family. Every small moment is worth it.

NOTE

1. Martin Gilbert, *The Second World War: A Complete History* (New York: Henry Holt and Company, Inc., 1991), 92.

CHAPTER 4

Ride with a Guide

The Mueller Park Trail can be daunting. The first hundred yards include a couple of rather steep uphill climbs that can completely drain the uninitiated. Also, the first mile of the trail is generally much steeper than the following 5.5 miles and has many blind corners that can be just as hazardous when traffic is light as they are on a more crowded day.

An experienced guide has knowledge and perspective. His guidance allows one to know when more demanding parts of the trail will be confronted and when it will ease up. I have seen individuals in otherwise excellent condition collapse in seizures of nausea on their first attempt by over-extending themselves during the first mile of the trail. A guide who knows the trail can help keep the difficult parts in perspective, thus preventing those who depend on his wisdom from becoming exhausted and discouraged or from losing hope. A thoughtful guide will direct you when to rest, when to take water, and how to tackle the trail to minimize wasted energy. He will also encourage those who follow and uplift them during difficult moments by giving them hope that they are progressing toward their goal or when the trail eases a bit just ahead.

Travel in the mountains should always be approached with respect. Weather conditions can change rapidly. The trail itself can change dramatically in its technical aspects depending on recent or current weather or the time of year. A switchback turn is very different in the fall, with wet slippery leaves on the ground or when muddy after a good rain, than it is during the dry part of the summer. Wet or muddy brakes perform very differently than dry ones. The temperature can also provide challenges. It is possible to experience everything from hypothermia to heat exhaustion on the same trail, depending on the circumstances and time of year.

This means that a person must know the trail and how it can change, given any set of circumstances. The first time I rode the trail, I was not properly conditioned for such a ride. However, my guide, Jonathan, was reasonably well acquainted with the trail and knew where a novice might need to stop to catch his breath along the way. He helped me pace myself and remain hydrated, and the result was love at first ride. I immediately realized that ride was a great workout without being a man-killer if a person were in shape and properly prepared. As I became more familiar with the trail and introduced others, I followed the example of my original guide. I recall introducing my son Howie to the trail when he was quite young. He has always been in great shape, but he didn't have a mountain bike at the time and had only a few gears. I was amazed how much just a little encouragement and a few well-timed breaks did to make the experience enjoyable for him. Now, of course, he would need to back way off the pedals for me to keep up.

One of the most dangerous aspects of the trail is restricted visibility due to the frequent blind corners and overgrown foliage. This makes the trail very different from almost any other I have ridden. Anyone using this trail must be constantly aware to avoid collisions or accidents caused by the changing aspects of the trail itself. This is especially true of those using it for mountain biking. A good guide will know when he is approaching a sight-restricted section and slow down; a really good guide will call out and provide information to anyone who may be out of sight. It does no good to know the trail if you don't do anything with the knowledge. A rider who knows the trail well but disregards that knowledge and showboats or continues at speeds that will not allow him to avoid an accident is simply foolish and a hazard to himself and others. That kind of rider should never be a guide.

It is a great blessing during this life to have many along the way that can guide us in proper paths and help us anticipate hazards, slow down, rest, or work harder at the appropriate times. Such guides can strengthen our knees when feeble or lift us up with hope when our hands hang down (Isaiah 35:3–4). Our Heavenly Father provides many who can help us in times of distress or warn us of danger or disaster ahead. We only benefit, of course, if we heed their advice and if we use our own talents, experience, and knowledge wisely. Such an important principle deserves one more example.

I have enjoyed scuba diving for over twenty-five years. During the 1980s, I had the opportunity to do quite a bit of diving in the Cayman Islands, a beautiful location for any activity but especially diving. The water is clear, most of the dives involve little or no current due to the reef surrounding most of the island, and the sea life is plentiful, diverse, and colorful. On one occasion I chose to go night diving with a friend. We joined about a dozen others, and the guide boat took us about a half mile off shore but still within the reef. At night there are many different creatures out: octopi, lobster, and the occasional free swimming moray or spotted eel. It is also interesting to see the parrot fish that blow bubbles around their bodies and appear to sleep vertically in the water. Your vision is restricted to the scope of your flashlight, for the surrounding water is pitch black. At night navigation is more important even though the dive boat will leave a bright light hanging underwater as a beacon to aid in returning to the boat. On this occasion, my friend and I swam about a hundred yards from the boat.

Clear water is not really clear with sediment and sea life suspended in the water and with the pitch black of night; at about 30 yards it is not possible to see the underwater light from the boat. We were careful to note the underwater formations so we could find our way back by bottom navigation. However, due to the amount of water (about 30 feet), we were unsure which way to return, so we surfaced to look for the boat. On my way up, I noticed that my flashlight could illuminate the bottom from about twenty feet above, but the light could not give me a view of the bottom for the last ten feet to the surface. We surfaced and located the direction of the boat, and then I told my friend that I would go first. I felt that I could keep a straight course for ten feet until I saw the bottom. Bottom navigation would be fairly easy from that point. I dove, and the plan was for him to follow. Before I got ten feet under the water, my dive buddy grabbed my fin and gestured that I surface.

After surfacing, he told me that immediately upon diving I curved ninety degrees away from the boat and would have headed off in the wrong direction. We determined to swim on the surface until we could see the underwater light hanging from the boat and then dive and follow it to the ladder.

I was absolutely certain when I dove into the dark that I could keep my orientation for 10 feet. When I did it, I felt that I had stayed exactly on course. The truth was that I had not, and we could have ended up even more distant from the boat, lost in the ocean. Fortunately my dive buddy was a good guide that night and corrected me. We then adjusted our plan and chose wisely to follow the surface lights until we could see the submerged lights, and we were fine.

We learned the lesson that at times we may be absolutely confident in our direction but may not realize how disorienting the situation is in which we are mired. Good friends, a spouse that is on the right track, or an inspired leader are placed in our lives for a reason. Sometimes our perspective is not sufficient to help us make course corrections. My perspective in this case was completely off. Heavenly Father has not placed us on earth alone. At various times during our lives, others have the perspective we do not; they can provide gentle direction that, if listened to humbly, will keep us on course in spite of ourselves.

We also have a powerful guide in the Holy Ghost, or Holy Spirit. He can enlighten and teach us of all things, many of which we cannot learn in any other way (John 14:26). On the trail there are often unexpected obstacles, rapid changes in circumstances, and surprise encounters with wildlife just as there are in life. Our ability to maintain open communication with the Spirit can allow us to avoid many of these difficulties. The Spirit will be our teacher and guide if we listen and are worthy of His presence. If we choose to disregard or rationalize such guidance, we do so at our own peril. Relying only on ourselves can work when there are no surprises, but it sets us up for a fall when there are. Paul taught that "the natural man receiveth not the things of the Spirit of God: for they are foolishness unto him: neither can he know them, because they are spiritually discerned" (1 Corinthians 2:14).

The world today seems full of those who have fallen into the "Thanks, God. I can take it from here" trap. They ignore guidance and personal revelation, thinking they already know. In fact, the most frequent statement we seem to hear uttered from childhood to adulthood is, "I know." In modern usage it often means, "I don't want to hear anything else from you." We most often utter this when being reminded of something we have become a bit careless about. My response to my children whenever they utter this phrase is, "I'm glad that you know, but I am interested in seeing if you *do*." It is doing something with what we know that matters.

Satan and his followers know, but they did not do. That was the difference between us and them and keeping our first estate (Jude 1:6). Knowing is meaningless if you do not use your knowledge with wisdom and practice it in action. Saying "I know" often cuts short a moment when we have the opportunity to receive needed guidance from those in authority such as our parents, grandparents, or spiritual leaders. Worse, it can prevent us from seeking guidance through humble prayer. The Spirit certainly cannot teach us through the interference of our own hubris.

Pop culture and convenient beliefs abound and are wholly insufficient; we must develop real conviction regarding God's plan, our own value, and the reality of Jesus's sacrifice and what it does for us to give us the strength to overcome the trials we all certainly will face at some point on the trail. James Russell Lowell, poet, diplomat, and Harvard professor, wrote in his contemporary essay on Abraham Lincoln, "The only faith that wears well and holds its color in all weathers is that which is woven of conviction and set with the sharp mordant of experience."[1]

Thomas Paine, an eighteenth-century American patriot, also emphasized the need for something more when he said, "These are the times that try men's souls. The summer soldier and the sunshine patriot will, in this crisis, shrink from the service of their country; but he that stands it now, deserves the love and thanks of man and woman. Tyranny, like hell, is not easily conquered; yet we have this consolation with us, that the harder the conflict, the more glorious the triumph. What we obtain too cheap, we esteem too lightly."[2]

This combination of consistent application of faith and conviction with experience produces true conversion.

A strong witness of the Holy Ghost and experience well absorbed are critical to those who seek to develop such deep conviction and true conversion (see Romans 8:16; 1 John 5:6; Hebrews 10:15). True conversion may then be described as testimony and knowledge put into action consistently and faithfully (Acts 3:19; Luke 22:32). Thus the truly converted individual becomes a new creature (2 Corinthians 5:17) capable of remaining steadfast himself and strengthening those around him. It is so much more than belief or knowledge.

Knowing you need to lift weights, for example, will not make you stronger; you need to do it consistently and faithfully. This is a simple truth. The Holy Ghost can help us prepare for portions of our personal trail that are much harder to identify or much more challenging than they appear. Those who are "faithful over a few things" (Matthew 25:21) when He manifests Himself unto them, and do not harden their hearts are given a promise that they will be a "ruler over many things" and enter into the "joy of thy Lord" (ibid.). Conversely, those who harden their hearts and turn away from God to follow blind guides set up by the devil and his children will discover there is no acceptable substitute: "Not every one that saith unto me, Lord, Lord, shall enter into the kingdom of heaven; but he that doeth the will of my Father which is in heaven. Many will say to me in that day, Lord, Lord, have we not prophesied in thy name? and in thy name have cast out devils? and in thy name done many wonderful works? And then will I profess unto them, I never knew you: depart from me, ye that work iniquity" (Matthew 7:21–23). Those who harden their hearts and fail to hearken to their spiritual and earthly guides cannot avoid falling into the very pit they dig for others (Psalm 9:15).

As we learn to access the Holy Ghost and follow our earthly guides, we will find the trail much easier and avoid much unnecessary first aid along the way.

NOTES

1. James Russell Lowell, "Abraham Lincoln," *ClassicAuthors.net*, http://lowell.classicauthors.net/abrahamlincoln/.

2. Thomas Paine, *The Crisis* (December 23, 1776), *ushistory.org*, http://www.ushistory.org/Paine/crisis/c-01.htm.

CHAPTER 5

Momentum and Practice

When I swam competitively in high school and college, I learned an important lesson that I relearned on the mountain single track ten years later. The lesson is profound, and those who have not experienced it think it sounds unfair and is almost like cheating. But of course it is not. The principle is that of momentum.

In the swimming pool, a swimmer discovers that as he masters the technical aspects of a particular stroke and improves his speed and conditioning, swimming actually becomes more efficient and easier. In other words, as a swimmer learns to become more hydrodynamic, he gets faster and can maintain that speed because of conditioning; his body actually approaches a more efficient plane on the water, which requires less energy. Yes, a fast swimmer uses less energy than a slower one, given similar effort. Many of us have seen novice swimmers struggle with heads-up breathing and leg and hip heavy swimming. This creates such drag that it is nearly impossible to make meaningful headway. By comparison, watching accomplished swimmers in high school, college, or Olympic competition as they efficiently move through the water is like seeing art in motion. It is not a coincidence that many swimming teams have a particularly fast swimmer nicknamed "fish."

The same is true with trail riding. As the rider's conditioning improves and he becomes technically solid, he can move up the trail with the same cadence in a lower gear and gain sufficient speed to allow many of the uphill portions of the trail to be negotiated with little additional energy other than a gear shift. I call this "rolling the hill" because it doesn't feel like you are climbing, but more like simply rolling over rises in the trail. In addition, rocky areas that jar the slower rider can be almost effortlessly skimmed over by the experienced, balanced rider with momentum. This is not to suggest that speed is everything. Out of control speed certainly is momentum, but that type of momentum makes a biker a hazard.

The ability to sustain controlled momentum is a result of conditioning and has to do with the combination of practice and wisdom. A great swimmer who doesn't work out cannot sustain his technique, regardless of his knowledge. A conditioned mountain biker who ignores changing conditions and obstacles ends up in an accident, the severity of which is dependent upon variables out of his control. In both these situations, the individual may tout his freedom to choose not to prepare, exercise good judgment, or condition when in reality he has dramatically reduced his freedom and ability to influence the outcome and ultimately becomes bound. Peter described the situation clearly: "While they promise them liberty, they themselves are the servants of corruption: for of whom a man is overcome, of the same is he brought in bondage" (2 Peter 2:19).

The requirement, then, is for us is to actively and consistently practice the basic principles we are taught by our guides (see chapter 4). These include sincere prayer and thoughtful study of the word of God. They include seeking to be involved in faithful service to others in addition to simply attending religious services. Having regular activities where family is brought together and setting aside time for daily family meals are additional ways we strengthen our ability to receive guidance. Family prayer and scripture study also provide significant additional power not available in personal study and prayer alone. These and other areas provide the basic nutrients for proper and wise spiritual growth. These daily and regular requirements condition your spirit and allow access to the Holy Ghost so that you may maintain momentum during times of trial and wisely exercise proper perspective and understanding of God's will.

How do we identify spiritual momentum? One indicator is the willingness of our heart and mind to seek and follow God's will. God made this clear to Solomon when He said, "Know thou the God of thy father, and serve him with a perfect heart and with a willing mind: for the Lord searcheth all hearts, and understandeth all the imaginations of the thoughts: if thou seek him, he will be found of thee"(1 Chronicles 28:9). He also made it clear for us through Paul, "Now therefore perform the doing of it; that as there was a readiness to will, so there may be a performance also out of that which ye have. For if there be first a willing mind, it is accepted according to that a man hath" (2 Corinthians 8:11–12).

Sadly there exist individuals who have served faithfully for decades only to become fatigued and participate less actively in the gospel. Such individuals often justify their lack of involvement because they feel the requirements of the gospel are too great or restrictive or because of some offense, which they claim they "will never forget or forgive." This frequently becomes rationalization for taking an easier path.

Of course, a person does not need to have served faithfully to decide to travel the easier road. There are many inviting trailheads to choose from that lead nowhere. A person can fill his life with busy activities or isolated inactivity that serve no productive purpose even though they may not be considered overtly harmful. However, it is only when we fill our lives with the highest and best activities toward our fellow man that our faith is fully expressed and true conversion is evident. In doing so, we build and maintain the necessary spiritual momentum to ultimately become the type of people we must be to be justified before God (James 2:14–26). In the end, our faith and our actions are less about what we do than who we are becoming. Too many in the world today are on a path to become little or nothing. It is a world of distraction, wasted time, and opportunities. Dallin H. Oaks, a modern-day jurist, law school professor, university president, and religious leader, stated, "Some uses of individual and family time are better and others are best. We have to forego some good things in order to choose others that are better or best because they develop faith in the Lord Jesus Christ and strengthen our families."[1]

The easier path in the long run, and usually in the shorter run as well, is the Lord's path. Those turning from the marked path find that, without the Spirit and the Lord's guidance, the trials of this world are simply too much for a person to surmount on his own (see preface). Further, there comes with this disconnection a loss of ability to clearly make decisions. Why? A person loses the ability to discern between God's advice, his own rationalization, and the world's direction. Satan is a master at producing such confusion. This is not a new problem. Isaiah prophesied, "Woe unto them that call evil good, and good evil; that put darkness for light, and light for darkness; that put bitter for sweet, and sweet for bitter!" (Isaiah 5:20).

Practice and mastery of gospel principles and Christlike attitudes require doing and being. Maintaining momentum requires practicing doing the right things. The right things consist of those correct principles taught from on high through personal divine guidance, seeking diligently to understand the word of God, and hearkening to the counsel of our religious leaders as they are inspired by the Holy Ghost (see John 16:13; 2 Timothy 3:16; 2 Peter 1:18–21). Robert Frost said it beautifully in an excerpt from his poem, "The Road Not Taken."

> Two roads diverged in a yellow wood,
> And sorry I could not travel both
> And be one traveler, long I stood
> And looked down one as far as I could
> To where it bent in the undergrowth . . .
> I shall be telling this with a sigh
> Somewhere ages and ages hence:
> Two roads diverged in a wood, and I—
> I took the one less traveled by,
> And that has made all the difference.[2]

When you choose to enter the strait gate and follow the narrow path, you are choosing the path "less traveled by." It requires vigilance, effort, and practice to negotiate it well. As you hold to the true course, you build spiritual momentum and find the rest God promised to Moses: "My presence shall go with thee, and I will give thee rest" (Exodus 33:14). Such a choice makes all the difference.

NOTES

1. Dallin H. Oaks, "Good, Better, Best," *Ensign*, Nov. 2007, 104–108.
2. Robert Frost, "The Road Not Taken," *Poets.org*, from the Academy of American Poets, http://www.poets.org/viewmedia.php/prmMID/15717.

CHAPTER 6

Awareness and Utilizing Gifts

I have looked forward for many years to putting the observations of this chapter on paper because they apply in so many situations. Riding along a narrow single track with drop-offs and limited visibility produces potential difficulties that are rarely encountered on wider trails or constructed paths. Even most single track mountain bike trails have much better visibility than is found at Mueller Park. This makes the Mueller Park ride beautiful, interesting, and sometimes unexpectedly hazardous. There are dozens of blind spots that exist just in the first 3.5 miles from the bridge at the trailhead to Big Rock. As stated, the trail can be busy and, even when it is not, it seems that just when a rider begins to feel he is alone on the hill, he rounds a corner and there's another person on his way up or down.

This situation requires constant awareness, knowledge of the trail or a good guide to know where the blind spots are, and the use of all your senses, especially your sense of hearing. I will focus on hearing and speech here, for these are often ignored by those on the trail and can mean the difference between a pleasant outing and an unpleasant incident.

With the digital age in full bloom, it is not uncommon to see a hiker, jogger, or even a biker with headphones or earbuds. While music or an audio book may make the trip more enjoyable, it puts them at a disadvantage. It can produce a situation that is hazardous for both the user and others. A person with both ears absorbed by such a device has diminished his auditory capacity. He cannot hear a bike approaching from either direction. If he also has his head down, he may have little or no advance warning even from the front. From the rear he is unlikely to hear a rider call out to him courteously or as a warning, and in many cases it is necessary to actually touch him on the shoulder to inform him that you would like to pass from behind. He certainly has little opportunity to hear another person coming from around the corner. This is difficult on the clear stretches of trail because so many hike, jog, or ride with their heads down, as mentioned. It is dangerous when approaching a blind corner.

Proper courtesy on the trail is to call out verbally when approaching a blind stretch and let people know you are approaching. If you hear such a warning, it is appropriate to respond by communicating back your status; let him know you're there. This is easy to do. If two are going the same direction, it is easy to let the slower traveler know you are coming well ahead of time so he can step to the side if necessary. These actions show both common sense and courtesy. Unfortunately, occasionally those on the hill treat it like a race course (read this as out of control momentum for the conditions or limitations of the trail) in both directions and compound the risk by not communicating and sometimes having earbuds in themselves. However, even a person using the trail at responsible speeds can have an accidental meeting if he ignores this advice.

Accidents occur each year because of failure to follow these simple, common sense rules of courtesy and safety. A person cannot deaden or disregard his senses and get very far on the trail. Deadening your sense of hearing going up the trail is like driving in the wrong lane on a curvy mountain highway without rearview mirrors. You are a danger to those in both directions. Doing so on the way down and compounding it by not communicating is like driving on a dark night with your lights off and your eyes closed. Both place your well-being and enjoyment out of your control and into a stranger's hands. You are at the mercy of circumstance in the hope that the stranger will exercise responsible behavior.

Some bikers have a bell, which is great in avoiding the surprise of an animal, but humans do not have such sensitive hearing, particularly around corners, and need information. Others say nothing even when communication is attempted.

Once on my way down the hill, I was approaching a particularly sharp turn with a more than 100-foot drop-off 12 inches to my right. I knew that just around the corner, anyone coming up would be struggling with the last few feet of the steep, rocky climb. I would probably have called out anyway, but I felt a particularly strong impression and called, "Biker coming, biker on the corner!" In the distance, I heard a tired voice: "I'm here." I slowed, and as I rounded the corner, I saw another biker struggling to get to a resting spot. He turned to me and simply asked, "How did you know I was there?" My response was, "I didn't; that's why I called out." He thanked me, and we both continued on.

An added courtesy is to remember that it is much tougher going up than going down. Those I ride with will stop and pull their bikes to the side to allow hikers, joggers, or bikers going up to do so without having to disrupt their own momentum. If the downhill rider cannot stop and pull over to the side for the uphill traveler, it is a sure indication that the downhill rider is not exercising proper control.

There is an obvious parallel in life. The world today is full of those things that would deaden our temporal and spiritual awareness. It is not accidently so. This deadening has been well described in its most extreme form by some who endured and survived concentration camps during World War II. In *Man's Search for Meaning*, Viktor Frankl wrote, "First . . . there was his [a new prisoner's] boundless longing for his home and his family. . . . Then there was disgust . . . with all the ugliness which surrounded him."[1] Frankl further states,

> "At first the prisoner looked away . . . he could not bear to see. . . . Days or weeks later things changed. . . . The prisoner stood . . . with his detachment. . . . He heard a scream and saw . . . a comrade . . . punished. . . .
>
> "But the prisoner . . . did not avert his eyes any more. By then his feelings were blunted, and he watched unmoved."[2]

The conclusion was that the prisoner entered a state of "relative apathy, in which he achieved a kind of emotional death."[3] While the situation Viktor Frankl found himself in was extreme, more subtle forms of this process of emotional deadening and death occur all around us.

I have known faithful Christians, some of which I have considered shining examples of the gospel of Jesus Christ, who have become entangled in such emotional deadening. At one point, they were active churchgoers, would never consider breaking a commandment, and were inspiring examples of service. However, somewhere along the line, they began to carry anger or offense in their hearts. They allowed the anger to fester because they felt they were some-how justified in not exercising Christlike forgiveness. Or, in some twisted rationalization, they convinced themselves that they were doing it for a righteous purpose.

Anger always has its own purpose, but it is never righteous, regardless of what we tell ourselves. It is tragic to see this anger turn into bitterness and then the cold millstone of hate. Such emotions not only mask an ability to receive spiritual guidance, but they also slowly push out all other desirable Christlike traits until wicked emotions are all that remain. It is heartbreaking to watch someone you care for slip into darkness and flirt with the damnation of his soul. As Paul said, "Let every soul be subject unto the higher powers. For there is no power but of God: the powers that be are ordained of God. Whosoever therefore resisteth the power, resisteth the ordinance of God: and they that resist shall receive to themselves damnation" (Romans 13:1–2). There is no shortage of counsel in the scriptures about the danger of anger, wrath, and rage. Job tells us that wrath has only the power to kill (Job 5:2), while James reminds us that it cannot produce righteousness (James 1:20). Paul states simply, "For God hath not appointed us to wrath, but to obtain salvation by our Lord Jesus Christ" (1 Thessalonians 5:9).

This is as difficult a trap from which to escape as any addiction because it starts quietly, feeding on itself, and its early stages can be masked and justified so easily. In addition, anger must have a focal point. Those engulfed often begin by focusing on the easier targets, more distant acquaintances, first. These targets can avoid or slip away, and over time, since anger must refocus, such individuals begin to target those that remain, ever closer relations. The entrapped soul gradually pushes away others until all that is left are the very closest relations who love and care and can help the most. Unfortunately, hate and anger are no respecter of relationships and continue to require targets. These closest and most loving of relationships are next on the list, and their ability to help is crushed. Their tragic choice is either to lose their identity and become an enabling sycophant or to be targeted. With no one left, Satan has the individual in a position to target themselves, with often tragic results. He is a master at getting those under such influence to dig a pit for their neighbor, which becomes their own prison (Psalm 9:15; 141:10; Proverbs 28:10; Ecclesiastes 10:8).

Anger and hate are a tragic foundation. They do not exist without self-deceit and selfishness. The process that has led countless individuals and civilizations to become separated from God by iniquity (Isaiah 59:2) and ready for destruction has always involved this at its very core. Jesus lamented the wickedness of the people in Jerusalem, saying, "O Jerusalem, Jerusalem, thou that killest the prophets, and stonest them which are sent unto thee, how often would I have gathered thy children together, even as a hen gathereth her chickens under her wings, and ye would not!" (Matthew 23:37; see Luke 13:34).

Jesus went on to prophesy of the destruction of Jerusalem and the sorrows of the last days, including our days: "For nation shall rise against nation, and kingdom against kingdom: and there shall be famines, and pestilences, and earthquakes, in divers places. All these are the beginning of sorrows. . . . And then shall many be offended, and shall betray one another, and shall hate one another. . . . And because iniquity shall abound, the love of many shall wax cold" (Matthew 24:7–12). He closes His prophecy by telling the disciples, "If that evil servant shall say in his heart, My lord delayeth his coming; And shall begin to smite his fellowservants, and to eat and drink with the drunken; The lord of that servant shall come in a day when he looketh not for him. . . . And shall cut him asunder, and appoint him his portion with the hypocrites: there shall be weeping and gnashing of teeth" (Matthew 24:48–51). The path for such behavior is and always has been the same—spiritual, physical, and ultimately literal destruction.

The secret to avoiding such hazards is, as on the single track, using our gifts and keeping open and positive communication. Prayer is the positive communication I speak of here. Prayer does two important things for us. First, it allows us to reach out to God and share our hopes, our fears, and our plans in a personal way. It allows us to recognize and express gratitude as well as seek assistance. Through it we can organize our priorities, commit ourselves, and report our progress. Second, it allows us to throw the gates of communication wide open, as we meditate and ponder, to receive pure and personal guidance in return. Such active communication, practiced with regularity, brings peace and strength. It allows us to better understand soul-saving principles and make additional strides in gaining an eternal perspective while dealing with life's many challenges.

In regularly seeking our Father in sincere prayer, we are promised that we will always have His Spirit to be with us, that we will receive gifts as necessary to accomplish the work we are placed here to do, and that we will, through such blessings, be able to stand and not faint when faced by even the gravest tests of this mortal existence. Truly the Lord spoke to us all when he said, "Ask, and it shall be given you; seek, and ye shall find; knock, and it shall be opened unto you: For every one that asketh receiveth; and he that seeketh findeth; and to him that knocketh it shall be opened" (Matthew 7:7–8). And further, "he that humbleth himself shall be exalted" (Luke 14:11).

This is one of the most difficult principles for youth in particular to appreciate. There is real power in prayer, as James tells us, "The effectual fervent prayer of a righteous man availeth much" (James 5:16). Too often our youth, and many adults for that matter, view prayer as a passing comment directed into space while we are on our way to somewhere else. Would you call your father on his birthday, speak a few words with little thought, and hang up? Of course not. But to some, this passes as prayer. God hears such words, but if he who prays doesn't care to approach his Heavenly Father with a sincere effort and an attempt at real communication and a meaningful relationship, he will reap what he sows—nothing. Prayer is powerful. It can produce blessings in our lives. It can save and heal us. It makes a difference. But if we deaden our souls to God, how can we hear His response or recognize His answer when it comes?

As we keep the lines of communication open to our Heavenly Father with regular, fervent prayer, we quicken our spiritual senses and enlighten our minds, thus allowing ourselves to avoid unnecessary difficulty. The added bonus is that, in spite of challenges that will still arise along the way, regular prayer keeps us close to Him and allows us to maintain a positive, faith-filled perspective. We will gain strength in overcoming the destructive traps that lead to anger, bitterness, and hate.

NOTES

1. Viktor E. Frankl, *Man's Search For Meaning* (New York: Simon & Schuster, Inc. 1984), 33.
2. Ibid., 33–34.
3. Ibid., 33.

CHAPTER 7

Sometimes You Hit the Rock Anyway

No matter how experienced you are on the trail or how conditioned you may be, bad things can still happen. They can have minor or major results. I remember riding up a particularly tricky portion of the trail. It is an uphill climb of perhaps 50 to 75 feet, and it is almost always slick because a spring trickles down the path. I was riding with a friend and got to the left of my usual line. There was a large rock with a cradle in front of it, which caught and stopped my front wheel immediately. I flew off my bike and cut my leg when I landed. I lay on the ground, bloody, dazed, and embarrassed. My friend rode ahead to make sure the path was clear and safe. After performing first aid to stop the bleeding and checking the various bruises and abrasions, I continued, thankful for my helmet.

On another occasion I was headed down the trail alone, about a half mile below Big Rock, peddling on an outside turn portion of the trail. Bikers tend to slightly point their toes downward as they pedal, and I was doing just that. There was a flat-sided rock sticking up a mere 3 inches from the trail floor, and my left toe caught the flat side. Since my toes were clipped in, it flexed my bike frame and literally catapulted me and the bike to the right, through some six-foot-high oak and into the air. I didn't come to a stop until my bike and I hit the slope about twenty feet below the trail and rolled another eighty feet down a steep rock fall. Lying at the bottom, I looked up and realized the incline was steep and there was no way out except to climb back up to the trail. Again, I had my helmet on and was well clothed, so abrasions and bruises were the extent of my injuries and my bike was miraculously unscathed. It took twenty minutes of inching my bike and my body up the slope and hanging onto tree branches to get back to the top. The rock is still there, and I have passed over it hundreds of times since. Each time I think about what happened and what I learned from it. And by the way, I have never since pointed my toes on that portion of the trail.

At times you cannot avoid a large root, log, or rock. Many times it is possible to hop or roll over them with only a slight loss of momentum. Other times, as described above, the result is more severe. On rare occasions tragedy can occur. We can approach such experiences positively by attempting to learn from them and perhaps be a bit wiser in the future. In order to have this growth, we must take responsibility for our part in whatever happens. This empowers us to further progress. It can also prevent recurrence of a nasty mishap. Cursing the root or rock certainly won't change its behavior.

Refusal to accept responsibility for our actions hampers spiritual progress in two ways. First, it sets us up as helpless victims rather than empowered children of God. By blaming others and trying to displace guilt for what happens to us, we reinforce in our hearts that it is not our fault and that we are victims. Some may develop the delusion that they had nothing to do with it as if they were simply innocent bystanders.

But if we had nothing to do with it, how can we avoid it again? Where will we be innocently standing next time a comet hits us? We are helpless, powerless, and eventually hopeless. Our life becomes full of continual offense, unfairness, and defeat. It can destroy our faith in God and our hope for a better future because we tell ourselves the lie that we cannot make a difference.

Second, it disallows learning. Why? Because it is not our responsibility. Rather it is the circumstance or something or someone else. Because we had nothing to do with it, we cannot overcome it. Therefore, there is nothing to learn unless we choose to become paranoid about all interactions. We become victims-in-waiting for the next calamity of life to befall us. Some people even become obsessed with watching for the next time life will take advantage of them, and when it does not happen, they fabricate an event or offense. Others are attracted to cultures that teach that the more they are deprived of or suffer, the better off they will be in the next life, so they seek out or manufacture gratuitous suffering. Still others establish a cult of fear inside themselves and also inside others they have influence over in a vain and selfish attempt to gain comfort through control over their own lives and the lives of others. This manufactured fear feeds on exclusion of people, places, and activities they believe are part of the offense, and in a misguided effort to protect themselves, they create their own prison.

I remember a young lady who would not participate in religious observance because she had been offended. She felt that the local congregation had ignored her at an important time in her life. She finally came back years later, and the congregation responded with love and attention. Unfortunately, she was offended again because she received too much attention and it made her uncomfortable.

A man I know has described his life as one long string

of faultless misadventures. Losing jobs, abdicating parental responsibilities, and choosing not to pay obligations that were due to the government, lenders, and God left him in a deep emotional and financial hole. In addition, disengaging his association with family and children left him with little, he was convinced, to live for. Yet, through it all, he continued to make the same thinking errors that placed him again and again in a position to fail.

Why doesn't he see it? Because he is a firm believer that life is against him. There is little he can do, and it's not his fault. The real tragedy is not what he has done to himself but what he has done to one of his sons, who has bought into his father's arguments that "life is unfair, so why try." This fine young man, still in his early twenties, has in turn struggled with motivation to make an effort to better his life and has sunk into endless online computer gaming, digital chatting, and other unproductive distractions. Several have attempted to provide counsel to the father, but he has slid so deeply into victimization and helplessness that he is simply unable to respond. Withdrawal and isolation do not make the demands of the world go away. Making up a pretend set of rules about how life should operate to suit you doesn't change things as they really are. Manipulating others into being loyal to your self-destructive cause only adds to the spiritual body count.

The gospel is not difficult to understand, nor is it mysterious. It is a message of love and kindness toward others combined with respect, appreciation, and love of God. Biblical writers, prophets, and the Savior himself spoke plainly of the path and the critical truths we must learn and follow to return to our Father's kingdom. Jesus taught, "If ye continue in my word, then are ye my disciples indeed; And ye shall know the truth, and the truth shall make you free" (John 8:31–32). That seems so clear. But the world is so full of noise, counterfeits, and appealing but empty substitute paths that we often wonder how we can identify the truth that will make us free. Paul saw our day and prophesied, "For the time will come when they will not endure sound doctrine; but after their own lusts shall they heap to themselves teachers, having itching ears; And they shall turn away their ears from the truth, and shall be turned unto fables" (2 Timothy 4:3–4). Is it not possible that Amos saw our day when he prophesied, "Behold, the days come, saith the Lord God, that I will send a famine in the land, not a famine of bread, nor a thirst for water, but of hearing the words of the Lord: And they shall wander from sea to sea, and from the north even to the east, they shall run to and fro to seek the word of the Lord, and shall not find it" (Amos 8:11–12).

How do we discern truth from fable, famine from feast? We have the answer: we continue in His word with patience, diligence, and faith, just as Caleb and Joshua did when Moses sent them to scout Canaan. The other scouts returned and spoke of a land rich with milk and honey but that "we be not able to go up against the people; for they are stronger than we. . . . All the people that we saw in it are men of a great stature. And there we saw the giants, . . . and we were in our own sight as grasshoppers" (Numbers 13:31–33). But Caleb responded in faith and said, "Let us go up at once, and possess it; for we are well able to overcome it" (Numbers 13:30).

It is tempting to sink deeper into the trap by manufacturing or manipulating ever greater real or imagined failures ("fables") to feed the demands of self-pity and helplessness. Why does this happen? There are at least two reasons. First, it is uncomfortable to take responsibility even though it usually is less so than we fear and the duration of difficulty is shorter than imagined. However, the easier path can initially appear to be playing the victim or ignoring our own responsibility in the matter. One of the issues here is often an insecurity in the position taken and eroded self-value. The "victim" can sometimes be seen attempting to manipulate others to his side in order to gain comfort or reinforcement for a behavior that, in his heart, he knows is a sham. Later, more pronounced behavior can then be driven by increasing insecurity, and campaigning often ensues. Children are often the targets of this as they become co-opted into the transgression through unwittingly enabling the parental campaigner by giving in to pressure to pick sides and demonstrate loyalty through appearing to support the influencer's abusive behavior. Sadly, the campaigner then uses these children caught in the middle by placing blame for his own behavior upon the children by professing that he did nothing to influence them and they made their own choices.

Second, one of Satan's most effective tools—and it has been from the beginning—is convincing a person to side-step responsibility for his own actions. Let's take a few examples of common excuses mankind has used throughout history and see them in a true light as an important tool in Satan's workshop.

I am not responsible for my acts because

1. There is no God. Therefore, there is no one to be accountable to, and God's law cannot exist. If there is no law, the concept of sin is false, and then there is no consequence for sin.
2. There is a God, but I have been saved or chosen. He is now in control of my life. Therefore, my acts are no longer my own. Sinful acts cannot be attributed to me.
3. There is a God, but fate controls everything. Therefore, there can be no personal accountability because my acts are all predetermined.
4. There is a God, but He is a disinterested entity with more important things to do. What happens here is of no consequence. We're on our own. Nothing I do matters to Him, so why bother?

5. It's not my fault. I was born with certain genetic predispositions that require that I act or control my acts in a certain way. It is unavoidable. I have no choice.

6. My environment is responsible—my circumstances, upbringing, disadvantage, or hardship. These have controlled my acts.

7. I ingested a substance that removed my ability to control my acts unexpectedly. The substance was therefore responsible.

8. I wasn't prepared or paying attention, I forgot, or nobody told me, so I didn't know what I was responsible for. How can I be responsible?

9. Someone told me to or made me do it.

10. He did it, so I can too. Or everybody does it or I didn't think. It's not my fault.

11. I am nothing, am of no consequence, have no value, and am invisible to others. What I do doesn't matter. Why should I try at all?

12. What I do only affects me or my body, so there should be no consequences.

13. The end justified the means, right? Life has been unfair. I am therefore entitled to get whatever I want to balance the scales.

In a very limited way and in certain circumstances, some of these may be justifiable. For example, we cannot be responsible for something we didn't know and didn't have an opportunity to learn. However, we cannot side-step responsibility because we refuse to accept or seek out understanding that is available. Regardless of the craftiness or seductiveness of these arguments or whether they are updated, popular, or hip, the result is the same. Satan seeks to deceive and have us avoid responsibility for our actions. Those caught in this trap seek to justify any behavior just as Cain, King Saul, and Pilate did (Genesis 4:1–16; 1 Samuel 15:24–25; Matthew 27:24).

Unfortunately, they often draw others with them.

Taking responsibility for our acts involves all the best Christlike qualities. It requires courage, repentance, and forgiveness. It builds trust in the Lord and faith and allows us to love God and our fellow men more fully. It allows us to reach out to our Heavenly Father through a veil of tears, feel His loving arms enfold us, and learn to more fully understand the grace embodied in our Savior Jesus Christ's great sacrifice. It gives us power to overcome trials, to learn, and to become wiser. But most of all, it is a practice field for the exercise of our freedom to choose and the divine concept of forgiveness of others. How? Because accepting responsibility opens the door to improvement through contrite repentance. And as we pedal up this difficult path, we gain understanding and insight as to the need for the Savior's Atonement and a greater appreciation of the incomprehensible gift of love that it is.

Forgiveness is the opportunity we have to exercise some small portion of the Atonement toward others. Paul defines this love of others like unto that which the Savior has for us and refers to this as the ultimate Christlike characteristic. "Charity suffereth long, and is kind; charity envieth not; charity vaunteth not itself, is not puffed up, Doth not behave itself unseemly, seeketh not her own, is not easily provoked, thinketh no evil; Rejoiceth not in iniquity, but rejoiceth in the truth; Beareth all things, believeth all things, hopeth all things, endureth all things. Charity never faileth. . . . And now abideth faith, hope, charity, these three; but the greatest of these is charity" (1 Corinthians 13:4–8, 13).

By taking responsibility for our lives and actions, we choose to empower ourselves. This enables growth and allows us to develop an appreciation of the Savior's great sacrifice as we turn to Him and feel His love. It leads us in the path to development of Christlike characteristics that will enrich our lives and uplift all those around us, the greatest of which is charity.

CHAPTER 8

Map Reading:
The Big Picture

Any mountain rider is wise to pick up a map or read one of the many trail guides prior to taking on a trail that is new to him. The more familiar you are with the trail, the less likely you are to get lost or into terrain that may be too technical or steep. A map, although lacking specific terrain detail, provides an important overview of the intended trip. However, a map is no substitute for an experienced guide, as you will see. I remember my first downhill ride on Baldy Mountain at the Sun Valley Ski Resort. I took my wife and four of our sons, anticipating an enjoyable afternoon of coasting and rolling. I am a map hound, so I studied a copy of the trail map and carried it with me on the ride. Unfortunately, the map was not sufficiently detailed to help us make better decisions along the way that would have improved our level of enjoyment.

The trip up the mountain via the ski lift was enjoyable and beautiful. The trail down had some unexpected uphill portions, and some in our group walked their bikes. But we stayed together and had a great time. Just as we were beginning to descend the Warm Springs switchbacks, we came to a fork in the trail and instead of continuing down the Warm Springs side, which looked a bit steeper on the map to me because of the frequent switchbacks, I led us on a trail back to the Baldy Face side. This was a mistake because it included a long traverse uphill. Everyone was tired by this point, and pushing a bike uphill is not a relaxing hike. After about half a mile of this, we came to some nice riding on a jeep trail that everyone enjoyed. The jeep trail turned into a cat-track that went straight down the ski run, which was an extremely steep slope of about 100 yards, ending at one of the ski lifts. We walked our bikes carefully down the hill and took the lift the rest of the way down to the car. We had an enjoyable ride, but had I been more familiar with the trail, I would have known that the Warm Springs side would have been much more enjoyable. I took my son and son-in-law that way the following year and learned the truth for myself. It was much faster and went right down to the parking lot.

Understanding the bigger picture while still picking up the critical detail is a must during our journey through this life. I had the opportunity to teach an adult scripture study class for a few years and came across a suggested activity that played out better than expected during one of the sessions. On this occasion, we were talking about the big picture overview of the entire gospel and how it helps us with perspective in this life. My family enjoys doing puzzles together and had recently completed a one-thousand-piece puzzle of the well-known painting of Jesus knocking at the door. I put all the pieces into three Ziploc bags and placed them out of the group's view. I had one puzzle piece in my pocket that was featureless and black. At the beginning of the session, I asked a good-natured friend of mine if he would help me with a demonstration. As things got underway, I called my friend to the front and asked him if he thought he was pretty good at doing puzzles. He explained he didn't do them that often but that he thought he could handle one. I then pulled out a black puzzle piece and handed it to him, telling him it was a true and accurate piece of one of our family's puzzles. I asked him to take as long as he wanted to examine it and then to tell me what the picture was that the puzzle piece was from.

He looked at the featureless piece for a moment and smiled as chuckles came from the group. He then thought he had me and said, "I can't do it." I asked why. He said that he needed the rest of the pieces of the puzzle and then he could answer. As he gave a satisfied glance at the rest of the class, I pulled out the three Ziploc bags from their hiding place, tossed them on the table, and said, "Okay, here are the rest of the pieces. Now tell me what the picture looks like." He looked at me blankly as the group broke into laughter and then simply said, "I need the picture." With the visual example fresh in everyone's mind, I allowed my friend to return to his seat and explained that there are several necessary steps to complete the puzzle. Only then will the entire picture become clear and complete. Here are the principles we discussed as they pertain to the puzzle and the gospel.

1. Many people have some true pieces, and some have many true pieces of the gospel. It may be possible to have all the true pieces, but like the bags of puzzle pieces on the table, it still does not help complete the picture. To successfully complete the puzzle you must have a sufficiently detailed map or picture as well as all the pieces.

2. Any new puzzle comes with a picture of what it looks like when finished. This is critical to

any progress and a must in understanding your overall objective and how everything fits together.

3. The complete gospel of Jesus Christ has all the pieces as well as the means to guide us (see chapter 4) in putting them together properly.

4. When putting together a large puzzle, a person is most likely to succeed by following these steps:

   a. Place the picture of the finished puzzle (sometimes on the box top) where it is visible and can be referred to. Then lay out all the puzzle pieces.

   b. Start with the edges so you can set the boundaries. This allows you to understand the limits of the puzzle and what space is part of the puzzle and what space is not.

   c. Build the areas that have easily identifiable features like faces, animals, trees, or buildings. This helps fill in the puzzle, but there will still be gaps.

   d. The puzzle then becomes harder as the solid colors and those with unclear features are worked on. A person must look at shading, slight differences in hue, and even grouping shapes of individual puzzle pieces. There is always a little trial and error, but the puzzle will come together.

The gospel has been revealed through ancient writers and prophets. Studying the gospel by the Spirit (2 Peter 1:18–21) allows us to set the boundaries for truth and separate it from the adversary's counterfeit worldly teachings.

As we learn "precept upon precept; line upon line" (Isaiah 28:9–10, 13), our knowledge grows and we are better able to pull together aspects of the gospel that are easily identified. These may include the basic doctrines, principles, personal obligations, and the framework of commandments we have been given.

As we continue to grow through obedience and faithfulness, we then are increasingly able to fill in the remainder of the gospel pieces through endurance amid life's experiences and as our minds are enlightened by the Holy Ghost. Understanding some principles more fully requires the test of time and exposure to challenges as well as prayerful study and obedience. Among these are principles for which we often pay a price; they include repentance, forgiveness, blessings that come from obedience, love, longsuffering, patience, and the interconnection of faith, hope, and charity. Throughout a faithfully lived life, full of service to our fellow man, we fill in the gaps and are able to understand more of the entire picture. We can see as we are seen, know as we are known, and ultimately be changed into the image of the Lord from glory to glory by the Spirit (1 Corinthians 13:12; 2 Corinthians 3:18).

Let's take an example of what missing one important piece of a puzzle can do to mankind's understanding of the big picture. Few in the world have real appreciation of the concept of Jesus Christ's Atonement and Resurrection. Careful study of the word of God gives us insight into this important principle. Think for a moment of the confusion that reigns because most of the world is missing just this one piece of the gospel puzzle. How can a person have any clear conviction about where we go after this life, the concept of why bad things happen to good people, the reason for suffering, the worth of individuals even if they are sinners, the concept of a loving versus a vengeful God, or why we are here at all? It is understandable that so many in the world would be confused about the purpose of this life, the value of an individual, the importance of marriage and family, the need for continuing guidance from God, their relationship with God, the true character of the Father and Son, and countless other lifesaving and comfort-giving doctrines.

On March 25, 2010, *Newsweek* reported on a series of surveys completed regarding the concept of resurrection. The results revealed that 80 percent of Americans surveyed said they believed in the concept of heaven. There is, however, little agreement on what, if anything, happens there. In fact, referencing several surveys, *Newsweek* reported that only 26 percent of Americans believed in a physical resurrection, while nearly 30 percent said they believed in reincarnation and 21 percent of those who professed to be Christian believed in reincarnation.[1] This intellectual and spiritual flabbiness can hardly be avoided when so much of the real picture is unclear and the adversary is working so hard to obscure it further by telling us the events described in the scriptures are not actual events but rather metaphors or symbolism. Modern-day religionists provide little assistance by side-stepping answers with the defense that these are great mysteries that man was not meant to understand, or simply buying into pop culture explanations.

As previously referenced, Amos prophesied that a time would come that there would be a "famine in the land . . . of hearing the words of the Lord" and that people could wander the land's length and breadth without finding His word (Amos 8:11–12). Is not this an accurate description of modern society?

Amos further counseled us that "surely the Lord God will do nothing, but he revealeth his secret unto his servants the prophets" (Amos 3:7). Are we to believe that God's work is done and He currently does nothing for humankind? The Savior expanded on this important concept by clarifying to Peter that the rock that is revelation did exist and must continue if the gates of hell are not to prevail (Matthew 16:17–18). To be clear, this references that for His organization and the gospel to prevail and continue, they must be built upon a foundation of revelation through a prophet as well as the right of each individual to receive personal revelation for guidance in his own life (Ephesians 2:20; 4:11–14). Clearly we have not arrived at a "unity of the faith" (Ephesians 4:13). Therefore, this should continue to be the case. There is no question that we certainly could use it. Only this continuing access and communication with God through the Holy Ghost, combined with sincere study of the word of God, allows us to complete key sections of the full gospel picture.

Throughout history good men have continued to rely upon God's revelatory guidance and sought to understand His ongoing will. They have wondered at the confusion and distraction of mankind. Gideon of old cried to the Lord when the Israelites were threatened by the Midianite armies, saying, "Oh my Lord, if the Lord be with us, why then is all this befallen us? and where be all his miracles which our fathers told us of . . . ?" (Judges 6:13). Gideon lived at a time we commonly view as being full of prophets and direct intervention from God. Yet, like many today, he wondered where God was and initially wondered, even while in the presence of an angel, if God had abandoned them. God in fact provided a miraculous response as Gideon, by following specific instruction, routed the Midianite army with only three hundred men, ushering in forty years of peace (see Judges 7:19–23; 8:28).

In 1838 Ralph Waldo Emerson delivered an address before the senior class of the Cambridge University Divinity School. He said,

> And it is my duty to say to you, that the need was never greater of new revelation than now. . . .
>
> . . . It is the office of a true teacher to show us that God is, not was; that He speaketh, not spake.

He also said, "Men have come to speak of . . . revelation as somewhat long ago given and done, as if God were dead."[2]

God, of course, is not dead. But we would assign Him the attributes of a disinterested God whose work with us is finished or even a nonexistent myth. Dr. Robert Gordon Sproul, president of the University of California system from 1930 to 1958, described essentially the same condition in modern Christian churches as did Emerson one hundred years earlier: "We have the peculiar spectacle of a nation, which to a limited extent practices Christianity without actively believing in Christianity. We are asked to turn to the church for enlightenment but when we do we find that the voice of the church is not inspired. The voice of the church today is the echo of our own voices. . . . The way out is the sound of a voice, not our voice. . . . It is the task of the pastors to hear this voice, cause us to hear it and tell us what it says. . . . Without it we are no more capable of saving the earth than we were capable of creating it in the first place."[3]

My son Neil has a device in his car that utilizes GPS (global positioning system) technology. It includes helpful maps and directions for virtually anywhere we wish to travel. No more fumbling with foldout maps or written directions; the computer voice gives us real-time guidance as needed until we arrive at our designated location. It is a great tool, especially for the directionally challenged. We were discussing this miraculous technology recently, and I asked two of my sons what the key benefit of the GPS device was in their opinion. They responded with the mapping application and the fact that "it gets you where you want to go." These are both important features, but I suggested that there was another feature that is more important, and without it the mapping and destination capabilities would be useless. After a moment of questioning looks, I told them the most important and basic feature is that it tells you where you are at any given moment (with a small error factor). Having a map and knowing your destination are meaningless if you don't know where you are on the map in relation to that destination to start with. So, with no place to begin, it is a meaningless instrument. However, because the GPS device automatically determines your location, all the other applications can run, and off you go.

A clear and complete understanding of the gospel with ongoing location and position capability in the Holy Ghost tells you where you are in relation to where you need to be. Continuing guidance is as critical to our spiritual progress as knowing where we are on the map when following directions. Because any movement spiritually, like when driving, changes your coordinates on the map, this guidance must be ongoing or it becomes imperfect and potentially flawed. It is not uncommon to pick up an old map, for example, and attempt to use it on a long drive only to discover that there are changes in the roads or road work that are not reflected. God has not forgotten us. He has not abandoned us during these troubled times. He is there and ever ready to give us a real-time response.

Believing that we lived with our Father before this life and that we made choices to come here is important. Understanding that this earth was created for our benefit and that we can become better people and return to our Father someday is also important. Appreciating that we are not insignificant specks of sand in the universe but are valued sons and daughters of God Himself makes a difference. Understanding that He has not left us alone but has promised to provide continuing spiritual guidance to us directly, as well as His promise that there would continue to be prophets, gives us confidence to carry on. The charge, then, is to avail ourselves of this direct access to our God through personal prayer and seeking this promised personal revelation. Our further charge is to seek out those who He promised would be the foundation of our faith, along with Jesus, who is the chief cornerstone, in this day and learn of them (Ephesians 2:20). This knowledge allows us greater perspective, just as a GPS and map do, so we cannot become lost and disoriented.

The world is full of questions, and a complete understanding of the gospel answers them. It provides a clear picture, an overall map. But our loving Father has not sent us out with a map and a picture and then left us alone. He has provided a comforter, even the Holy Ghost, as a daily guide through the detailed terrain of our individual path (John 14:26). He has, through Jesus Christ, provided an atoning sacrifice that we might overcome our mistakes and recover from taking a wrong turn (see 1 Corinthians 5:7; Hebrews 10:10, 12). He has also provided the scriptures and continuing revelatory guidance so that we can become fully converted, strengthen each other, and develop selfless, Christlike love through serving each other (Luke 22:32; John 15:12–13).

Recently I was in the home of an elderly woman who had asked me to give her a blessing before a rather serious operation. Her daughter was present, and I was impressed that she was burdened with something unspoken and also needed a blessing (James 5:14–15). I asked if she would like one. She answered, "I can't. I have things to work out." I felt an outpouring of God's love for her and witnessed to her of her Father in Heaven's love for her, regardless of any mistakes she had made or whether she had paid any attention to Him over the years. I told her that He was always there for her and that blessings were for all of us, flawed as we are, to strengthen us and let us know of our importance to Him. She again declined with the same words. I have thought much about the missing pieces in her life and how others can help her find and pull them together again. The Savior said of Himself, "I lay down my life for the sheep" (John 10:15) and "I am the resurrection, and the life" (John 11:25). His sheep are not just those who are doing all they can to be faithful, but his flock includes us all, that we might not also have to suffer if we follow Him.

The Apostle James promised us, "If any of you lack wisdom, let him ask of God, that giveth to all men liberally, and upbraideth not; and it shall be given him" (James 1:5). Jesus reiterated this promise when he taught, "Ask, and it shall be given you; seek, and ye shall find; knock, and it shall be opened unto you: For every one that asketh receiveth; and he that seeketh findeth; and to him that knocketh it shall be opened" (Matthew 7:7–8).

Use the map you have been given to pull together the pieces of the most important picture in your life. As you move forward, continue to seek personal guidance from God to be sure of your position on that map and approaching requirements. Know that you are loved and that there is always a hand there to lift you up if you will but look. He knows us and our situation and wants us to succeed.

NOTES

1. Lisa Miller, "Far From Heaven," *Newsweek*, March 25, 2010, http://www.newsweek.com/id/235418.

2. Ralph Waldo Emerson, address delivered to the Cambridge, MA Divinity College, July 15, 1838, *RWE Institute—The Works of Ralph Waldo Emerson*, http://www.rwe.org/works/Nature _addresses_2_Divinity_School_Address.htm.

3. Quoted in Howard W. Hunter, "Spiritual Famine." *Ensign*, Jan. 1973, 64.

CHAPTER 9

A Sense of Humor and a Good Pace

Biking on the local trail is usually a nice social experience. People are friendly and encouraging. If I have a mechanical problem or mishap, others are quick to offer assistance. There also are usually a few friendly people at Big Rock with whom to chat. This makes the exertion and obstacles along the way more pleasant. It is not uncommon to have another rider or two arrive at Big Rock feeling tired. One may even express frustration that the ride was much more difficult than anticipated. My response is usually to make room for them on the bench, offer encouragement, and remind them that anyone who can sit on that bench on a Saturday morning has accomplished something and should feel pretty good. It doesn't matter how long it took to get there.

As previously mentioned, mountain rides at a 5,000- to 7,000-foot elevation can present very different challenges, depending on the weather. Some conditions can be fairly miserable, like rain or snow. Others can be refreshing, like a cool canyon breeze on a hot day. The Mueller Park Trail is quick to recover from heavy precipitation. It dries out rapidly, although there are always a few lingering puddles and a couple of rather technical muddy slopes on the way up to Big Rock.

A few years ago, I bundled up because it was raining, and it continued to drizzle slightly for the first half of the ride. A small rivulet ran down the center of the track in many places. Because the trail has much undergrowth near and hanging onto the trail, it is not possible to avoid brushing against the water-laden branches and leaves. This will soak your clothes quickly. On this day I expected such a result, so I layered up and wore an extra Windbreaker. The ride was sloppy, muddy, and wet. By the time I got back to the trailhead, my entire front from head to toe was covered with splatters of mud and dirty water. I had no fender on my front tire, so I became a human mud flap. I must say I was miserable and soaked through all my layers by the time I crossed the bridge to the parking lot.

As I stopped to consider my plight, I noticed an athletic-looking college student preparing to start her ride. She couldn't have looked more out of place. She was dressed in a newly washed white T-shirt and sweats with nice, clean white socks and even white running shoes. I know how difficult it is to get mud splatter stains out of white clothing, but I said nothing. She looked up at me. I must have looked like something out of a 1950s "B" movie with the words *Swamp Thing* in the title. She simply said, "So is it muddy up there on the trail today?" I was dumbfounded at a question that was easily answered with a glance. I hesitated a moment, considering how to respond, and then said, "Oh no, it's perfectly dry." We both broke out in uncontrollable laughter. Suddenly being the inside of a fender didn't feel so terrible.

A good sense of humor does not mean tearing down others or being crude. It does not require a person to engage in off-color stories or profanity, and it certainly does not include making light of sacred things. These things are, in fact, not humor at all. Life seems to present situations that give us opportunities to lighten our burdens and raise our spirits.

A sense of humor is an art based in remaining cheerful and obtaining and using the spiritual gift of finding joy and wonder along the path. The Lord reminded His disciples frequently that even in the most difficult times they should "be of good cheer" (Matthew 14:27; Mark 6:50; John 16:33; Acts 23:11), and Paul taught us that "God loveth a cheerful giver" (2 Corinthians 9:7). Jesus said that even in the most daunting moments, "These things I have spoken unto you, that in me ye might have peace. In the world ye shall have tribulation: but be of good cheer; I have overcome the world" (John 16:33). Moses taught the same truth, "When thou art in tribulation, and all these things are come upon thee, even in the latter days, if thou turn to the Lord thy God, and shalt be obedient unto his voice; . . . he will not forsake thee" (Deuteronomy 4:30–31). The better we understand how valuable we are to our Heavenly Father—how much He has done for us and how much He desires to bless us further—the easier it is to find enjoyment and maintain our cheerful outlook and wholesome sense of humor, even during the darkest of times.

As my friends and I get older, it seems there is an increasing number of spiritual and physical challenges in our lives. In our twenties, we talked about sports. Later our conversations were about our children and families. Nowadays we talk increasingly on our operations, aches, and maladies. I know—it sounds pathetic to me too. Some of these challenges can be overcome, but others require adjustments in behavior and lifestyle. A few are life threatening, and some break your heart. I recently visited a good friend in the hospital; he is now retired after thirty-six years as the local fire chief. He has been physically active but since his retirement has experienced a series of disheartening medical setbacks. On this occasion, blood clots had lodged in his lungs.

I was concerned that I would find him discouraged. Upon entering his space in the emergency room, I was greeted by a cheerful hello. We had an uplifting conversation, and I was impressed that he had maintained his positive outlook on life. We discussed his situation, and he and his sweet wife kept up a conversation back and forth that reminded me more of a relaxing Saturday afternoon on their back porch than sitting behind curtains in the ER. The high point was when he told of taking his oldest son (who is now a fireman himself and arranged for the paramedics to transport his dad to the emergency room) to the fire station a number of years before. His son was young and excited and enjoyed the day. However, on the ride home, he seemed disappointed. My friend recalled asking his son what was wrong. The boy turned to his father and said, "Dad, I was hoping to see all the clowns you have always said you work with."[1] We laughed, and it brightened all our spirits.

The built-in calamities of life on this earth, the very nature of growing older and having children, who in turn grow and multiply, bring with them many severe tests. Some people approach life wound so tightly that every little thing becomes big. They have nothing left when something really big occurs. I worked for many years in one of the most intense professions imaginable, that of investment banking. Pressure to perform was constant, competition extreme, and expectations always extraordinarily high. I watched as many of my peers' priorities became altered and their pace frenzied. It was tragic as so many good men and women fell by the wayside or were crushed under the mounting stress simply because they had not given sufficient place for faith and hope. Therefore, they took it all so seriously and could not enjoy the process. Worst of all, some were unable to laugh at themselves or their situations when that could have been the best medicine. Of course a person's occupation is important, as is his faith and his family. But we cannot become so intense that we break ourselves against the challenges of life. I have found that a sense of humor, the ability to find that which is good and uplifting along the way, and the capacity to keep a healthy perspective about the trail and my priorities have made a big difference in my ability to endure.

So what was the difference? Some have an ability to bring cheer regardless of the circumstances. Others are able to maintain a healthy and hopeful outlook because they have balanced their lives. Yes, they may have stress in their jobs or family, health or financial concerns, or other problems, as do we all. But their focus on their family and their relationship with God, their understanding of the Savior's sacrifice for them, and the blessings that come from giving to others are all critical to keeping life's stressors in perspective.

Years ago my mother lived next door to a gentleman who had survived the Bataan Death March and years of captivity in Japanese prisoner of war camps during the Second World War. He wrote a book describing his experiences, and I was given a signed copy. He made this observation about those who survived the incomprehensible trials versus those who didn't.

> It was a gut-wrenching experience when cleaning up after a death, to be watched by ten or fifteen pairs of glazed eyes and have someone say, 'Lieutenant, you can do that for me tomorrow.' I knew that it would happen. Most often the illness would be real, but sometimes it was just a case of giving up; the will to live had been lost. There was nothing more I could say or do to help, and I have lived with the frustration of that failure ever since. . . . There I learned another survival skill: the control of depression, perhaps more insidious and lethal

than the diseases with which we were now so familiar. Everyone was affected by it to some degree and it took a conscious and continuous effort to overcome. Never allow the overwhelming daily stress to obscure the ultimate goal. Immerse ones' self in helping others where possible, realizing that in so doing, personal psychological problems are minimized to the point that they are bearable. Search always for the bright side of any situation, even though its light may be very dim most of the time. This approach, partly deliberate and partly instinctive, was vital to the preservation of mental and physical stability. I could sense it in myself and observe it working for others, who almost always were the ones contributing to the general welfare of the camp.[2]

We don't have to look in such extreme situations to find such strengths and weaknesses among us. The world today seems to be full of "can't do" attitudes. Pop culture seems, on the one hand, to encourage us to do whatever feels good without any limits. On the other hand, when a person desires to make something of himself or achieve some great benefit for mankind, the streets seem to be lined with crowds discouraging the effort. The public chant seems to be, "It can't be done," "Don't waste your time," "We have to learn to lower our expectations," or simply, "It's not worth all the effort." With so many easy diversions available that take no effort, learning, or commitment, it is tempting to avoid setting and achieving goals or correcting any problems you may have. However, the gospel of Jesus Christ is a "can do" philosophy. The Savior made it clear that nothing is impossible; anything can be accomplished as long as we work at it with God as part of our team (see Matthew 19:26; Mark 10:27; Luke 1:37; Luke 18:27).

The person who uses up all his energy fighting the hill with every rotation of the pedal is the perfect example of first mile burnout. Life is not about who races ahead at the start; it is about getting to the goal prepared and ready to move on. The person who can maintain a positive outlook and takes time to learn the skills that will allow him to do so will still be on the hill pumping long after others have turned around and headed back.

NOTES

1. Personal conversations of the author with Brent Argyle, February 2010.
2. Thomas R. Harrison, *Survivor* (Salt Lake City: Western Epics, 1989), 164–65.

CHAPTER 10

Shepherding:
Riding with Others

O ne of the best ways to experience mountain biking is with friends. The camaraderie is enjoyable; sharing the experience with others makes it richer. I have also learned new things about the trail and about my friends when taking them up the hill for the first time. There are several keys to making this kind of experience memorable and positive.

Group Organization: If there are more than two riders, it is important to place the more experienced riders at the front and the back of the group. This allows the rider in front to anticipate danger spots, difficult stretches, or rest intervals and communicate as necessary. The rider in the back can also talk to the front rider to keep the proper pace, warn of faster riders coming from behind, or notify the leader if members in the group need a break. Unfortunately, I have seen groups of riders or hikers strung out all over the trail with their experienced leaders in the front only. These leaders would have no idea if one of the group members got into trouble. Large groups should not be attempted unless they have sufficient experienced riders to split into several more manageable groups.

Speed of Travel: It is critical to move at the pace of the slowest rider. It is common to see a group of four or five riders doing the opposite. The first couple are usually well conditioned and moving rapidly. But the last couple of riders might as well be riding alone and do not appear to be enjoying the trip. The uphill ride can be discouraging enough if left behind, but with drop-offs to the right most of the way, going down can be even more disconcerting for a novice. In addition, all the braking that is required can quickly fatigue a novice's hands (see chapter 13). If you start as a group, you have made a decision to be a group, so stay together.

One hot summer day when I was riding down the mountain, I stepped to the side as two fast, experienced riders raced past going up. I then pulled back on the trail and continued downward. About a mile down the hill from where the two fast riders passed me, I came upon a young lady who was obviously struggling and was walking her bike. It was clear she was made up for a date, but at this point her hair was mussed and sweat was coursing down her cheeks. She seemed quite distressed, so I stopped to see if everything was all right. I learned that she was with one of the speedsters and had not seen him since early in the ride. She was *not* a happy camper, and it was easy to imagine that the speedster would not get a second date. Fortunately she was uninjured; much worse could have happened to someone like this who was unfamiliar with and unprepared for the trail. It is not only selfish but also irresponsible and dangerous to leave the weakest members of your group to fend for themselves.

We also work in groups to progress during this life.

Family is, of course, the most important group, but we also have neighborhoods, congregations, service groups, classes, teams, troops, departments, and friendships. These groups should bring strength and support to those who are actively involved and should reach out to those who are not. The family is the group I will focus on to illustrate the point.

A family has the two most experienced members (mother and father) leading and following up on the other members' progress during life. This is much more difficult when one of the parents is not present or when the parents are not on the same page. Members of the family may move at different speeds at different times in their lives. It is also true that teenagers may chafe under the concept of parental shepherding. Youth, trials, personal faith, ignorance, and transgression can all affect family members along the way. At these times they need their experienced leaders most, but so often this is when they are left without the help that Heavenly Father placed there for this very purpose. As parents, we cannot allow self-indulgence, distraction, fear of reaction, lack of faith, or misplaced priorities to prevent us from fulfilling those responsibilities we understood and agreed to before coming to this life.

I recall a pleasant social visit with my neighbors. The couple had not developed any personal or organized religious values or patterns. The conversation turned to spiritual matters, and it became clear that they were concerned about their ten-year-old daughter. She was beginning to show signs of an at-risk youth through her push toward independence and desire to dress, act, and hang out with older kids, including boys. We talked of gospel values and involvement in some church organization where she would be exposed to such teachings. They had been attempting to teach their daughter some values but had little in their own background to aid them in the process. They were interested but later decided to opt out because it took too much time away from their own pursuits and interests to provide real parenting to their daughter. Their excuse was that they were going to wait until she was sixteen and then let her choose for herself. What a tragedy! They may look back one day and discover that their opportunities to influence her in righteous paths occurred well before she turned sixteen and without ongoing, consistent influence, she would certainly not have the foundation upon which to make wise choices in high school. This selfish parental choice could not only curse the parents' and daughter's lives for many years, but it could also divert their descendents upon strange paths. Parents can make decisions that run through families, for good or bad, for generations.

A wise man, and one of my mentors, once told me that selfishness is at the root of all transgressions. I have pondered that for many years and have concluded that such a statement is hard to refute. In the Gospel of Matthew, the Savior is asked by a clever lawyer, in an attempt to lure Him into a controversial stand, which of all the commandments was the greatest in the law (Matthew 22:35–40). The Savior's response confounded him, "Thou shalt love the Lord thy God with all thy heart, and with all thy soul, and with all thy mind. This is the first and great commandment. And the second is like unto it, Thou shalt love thy neighbor as thyself. On these two commandments hang all the law and the prophets" (Matthew 22:37–40).

If there are two great commandments, then it follows that there must be two great sins. The first would be putting something else before God—known as idolatry. The second, then, must be like unto it, and that would be to love yourself more than others. Sounds like selfishness to me. So it follows that the great sins become idolatry and selfishness. In fact, idolatry is, in effect, putting your own vain desires before God, which could be seen as a form of selfishness. So the two sins may be combined into one great sin of selfishness. To finish the parallel, we would conclude that upon these great sins hang all the other sins and transgressions.

I recall an example of this on the trail and how it has now turned around. Nineteen years ago on a trip to Sun Valley, Idaho, I had my first exposure to serious mountain biking. My sister and her husband invited my wife and me to join some friends on what I now know is one of the most challenging mountain biking loops in Sun Valley, the Adams Gulch Loop Trail. It is a 7-mile loop involving a 1,100-foot climb that requires another 5 miles each way from the resort to the trailhead and back. We took our oldest son, Travis, with us, who at the time was about eleven. He has always been a superb natural athlete, but this was a long, steep ride.

We rode a few miles from the resort and up a canyon to the north of the Warm Springs side of Baldy Mountain. The trail up the canyon was enjoyable, and we crossed the stream several times, which is always fun. We then turned and began a serious climb up steep switchbacks. About a third of the way up the steepest portion, my son was unable to ride further. He pushed his bike around another bend, and then it became clear he really needed assistance. I put his bike on my shoulder and carried it while pushing my own bike in front of me. It was slow going, but we made it up that steep portion, and by then he was refreshed and was able to continue the rest of the ride, which from that point was very technical but also mostly downhill.

The view from the trail summit was spectacular, and it was a great blessing to share it with him. The bonus was that by helping him along the way, his attitude stayed positive and he fully appreciated the beautiful views that came later. We have since ridden together on a number of trails in those mountains as well as in Utah, and now he must slow down to make sure he doesn't leave me behind. He has become a wise trail guide himself and would not hesitate to carry my bike if the need arose. The moral of this story is that sometimes it is not enough just to lead; at times we must help shoulder the burdens of those in our flock, for they are too great for them to bear alone. This is true also in our effort toward God-fearing leadership. At times we must turn to Him for help in bearing our own burdens. He is always there and will respond.

Parenthood requires selfless sacrifice of your time, talents, and resources to bring your children to the point of partaking of the fruit of God's love (Proverbs 11:30; Matthew 7:16–20). I cannot read the Savior's words regarding children without them touching tender emotions as I imagine the scene. "Then were there brought unto him little children, that he should put his hands on them, and pray: and the disciples rebuked them. But Jesus said, Suffer little children, and forbid them not, to come unto me: for of such is the kingdom of heaven" (Matthew 19:13–14; Mark 10:13–14; Luke 18:15–16). Mark and Luke include an additional statement by the Savior: "Whosoever shall not receive the kingdom of God as a little child shall in no wise enter therein" (Luke 18:17; see Mark 10:15).

Can you imagine taking one of your children to meet the Savior, hoping for the opportunity and the impact it would surely have on their lives? Imagine facing the opposition from those who think they are protecting the Savior. Then as your children are called forward, tears of gratitude water your eyes. As the Savior blesses them, you fall to your knees in wonder. You look at these innocent children as you absorb the lesson that you must become like them and commit yourself to do all you can to preserve their virtue and build in them a righteous purpose. What would you talk about on the way home and at pivotal moments later in their lives? Would this steel your spirit and your determination to do all you can?

This too is our charge. We are to do all we can with those for whom we are shepherds. They know our voice, and most will choose to follow. Sometimes they will mistakenly put their trust in those who lead them down strange paths. Your contact with them may even be severed for a time.

Regardless of physical, emotional, or spiritual distance, we must continue to seek after our sheep.

Then, upon the return of the prodigals, we encircle them in the arms of our love, allow them to feel God's love, and help them move forward. This is exercising the pure love of Christ, which is charity. It does not keep score but is willing to suffer for a long time. It is kind, it does not envy, it is not prideful, it is meek and lowly in heart, it is not selfish, it is patient and not easily provoked, it gives the benefit of the doubt and thinks or dwells not on evil or the negative, it rejoices in truth and righteousness, and believes and hopes all things (1 Corinthians 13:1–8, 13). Because of this, charity can endure all things and never fail. Of course, it requires great effort to develop. John reminds us further to appreciate the love our Heavenly Father has shown us as he says, "Behold, what manner of love the Father hath bestowed upon us, that we should be called the sons of God. . . . Beloved, now are we the sons of God, and it doth not yet appear what we shall be: but we know that, when he [the Savior] shall appear, we shall be like him; for we shall see him as he is. And every man that hath this hope in him purifieth himself, even as he [the Savior] is pure" (1 John 3:1–3).

Do all you can to keep your group together. Do not become distracted by vain pursuits or wounded pride, or give your heart over to selfishness, dark thoughts, or anger. These are the opposite of the love of which John and the Savior spoke. The Savior himself tells us still today, "Come unto me all ye that labor and are heavy laden, and I will give you rest" (Matthew 11:28). As we do this, we are promised that the Savior's yoke is easy and His burden is light and that we will be strengthened to bear the burdens that are placed upon us (Matthew 11:29–30). In so doing, in time, you will bring your flock safely home, and great will be your joy with them in life eternal (Luke 15:6–7).

CHAPTER 11

Know Your Personal Limits

Knowing our limitations is always important. However, there are three times when personal limits must receive special attention on the Mueller Park trail. First, the early spring riding period. The weather is unpredictable and careful preparation is important, but the more important factor is that most of us do not maintain our conditioning at as high a level during the winter as we do at other times of the year. It is possible for the heartiest of riders to move to road biking and ride during the high mountain winters or to have a regular aerobic indoor alternative. However, human nature and the cold weather make this difficult to maintain. Northern Utah is a wonderful place to live if you want to have a legitimate winter but you don't want to have too much. The Wasatch Front typically has about eight to ten weeks of what I consider frigid weather (twenty degrees and below). Interspersed are several weeks of Indian summer, where the temperatures can rise to the thirty-to-fifty-degree range. This really isn't too bad as winter goes and allows for reasonably pleasant road riding if you dress properly.

The trail to Big Rock is mostly clear of snow by late April, so mountain biking can resume. When resuming regular rides in the spring, it is important to understand that you will be working at a slower pace than you were at the end of the previous riding season when your conditioning was at a peak. To avoid early setbacks like pulled muscles, it is best to work gradually back up to an adequate level of conditioning.

Second, riding at the end of the fall has many of the same weather-related issues as early season riding. These, again, have to do with dressing properly and particularly protecting your fingers, ears, and face. This has been discussed previously and will not be addressed again here. Spring and fall riding can also involve slogging through soft or muddy ground, which takes more energy and slows your overall rate of travel. This can also require careful management of your energy usage and water intake during a ride.

The third situation where you must know your limits is perhaps the least obvious when you are riding. It is the midsummer period when high temperatures can wear you down. On a hot day it is best to ride early, before the temperature rises, but that is not always convenient. As a result, the trail can have rather heavy usage during the warmer morning hours and then again in the later afternoon when the angle of the sun is better but the ground still radiates heat. If you choose to ride the trail during a warmer period, be sure to hydrate before you begin and continue to drink liquids during your ride. At times I have not hydrated sufficiently or it has been warmer than anticipated. The heat doesn't bring a rider down all at once; it is a subtle attack. You may notice your bike seems just a little bit squirrely or you are weaving a tiny bit and your balance is slightly off. There can be a dizzy, light-headed feeling as if you had hyperventilated. Should you notice these symptoms, it is a good idea to find a shady, cooler spot (usually on an inside bend or near a stream by one of the bridges), cool down, and hydrate. After a rest and some water, it might be wise to consider turning around and riding down. You are close to your personal limit for that day.

I will add one more special case. I have occasionally taken a friend from out of town up the trail. If the individual has come from low elevation, one of the coasts, for example, it is important to use additional discretion due to the change in altitude and his inability to properly acclimate. The result for the careless is a case of early stage burnout and need for a long afternoon nap for the uninitiated rider. Any type of exhaustion, dehydration, or fatigue has accelerated effects if a dramatic change in elevation is added to the mix.

Life can also sneak up on us sometimes, and we find ourselves spiritually disoriented and out of balance. The principle I will emphasize here is one taught to me by one of my most influential religious leaders, Allen C. Rozsa, during my exit interview at the end of my two-year gospel proselyting mission in 1977. The perspective gained has been critical in managing during several periods of my life when spiritual threats were subtle but nonetheless real.

He taught me about the principle of "spiritual vertigo."[1] Before explaining the principle, some background is necessary. Allen Rozsa came straight to his assignment as leader of the ecclesiastical mission in which I served after a career as an Air Force pilot. He flew during World War II, the Korean Conflict, and the Vietnam War. He had flown a wide variety of aircraft, producing many inspirational stories, and the missionaries loved to get him on the subject during our staff meetings. He was one of my personal heroes. I loved him and his wife with all my heart. They are the two people that have been, and remain today, the most influential in my life. They welcomed me as part of their family, and I still feel that to this day. On this occasion, he counseled me in preparation for my return home from full-time service. I had completely immersed myself in gospel service and believe now that he recognized that those who had done so needed a little extra preparation for effective transition to the next stage of their lives.

Allen counseled me to beware of "spiritual vertigo" and explained that one of the greatest dangers in flying was losing perspective regarding where you are in space and not relying on your instruments to help you get back on track. He asked me to think of taking off in a jet airliner. The acceleration and lift as the jet climbs is obvious. Then the rate of ascent decreases as the aircraft approaches its cruising altitude. The occupants experience the feeling of acceleration at takeoff and the steep climb and can mistake the decrease in the rate of ascent for descending. In fact, the aircraft is still gaining altitude but at a lower rate, and the human senses are deceived into feeling the aircraft is losing altitude. Allen then explained how dangerous this can be for a pilot at night or in clouds when there are no visible points of reference.

He then related this to my situation. He warned me that I had been immersed in something so completely and had been growing spiritually on such a steep curve that when I returned to home, school, and regular life, I could develop a feeling that I was losing my spiritual connection when, in fact, I was continuing to grow but at a lower rate. He went on to explain that new converts following their baptism can also go through a period where they struggle spiritually. An early opportunity to serve, continuing instruction, and study can be helpful in these situations. Over the years I have discussed this subject with those who have recently returned from similar service, those who have completed their assignments as religious leaders, as well as a variety of others who have completed less visible assignments (but that took everything they had to effectively perform) and found no exceptions. I remember one returned leader telling me that the eighteen months immediately following the completion of his full-time service was one of the toughest transitions of his life.

Sometimes such periods can occur as a result of one of the great trials of your life. The loss of a close family member on whom you have depended, serious illness or injury, financial upheaval, or a disruption in the family unit can bring about such vertigo or even a period of free fall.

Those who experience "spiritual vertigo" know well the feeling of steep spiritual growth and sense a change. It can be frustrating, almost like hearing an amputee talk about still being able to feel his missing appendage and having an itch that cannot be scratched. These intensely spiritual experiences are foundational in your life.

One who gives all he had to his service and finished with honor, knowledge, and faith as Paul advised (1 Corinthians 9:24) should not be surprised that his growth might level off a bit. It then becomes his responsibility to recognize that growth is continuing. It continues in part by overcoming the very challenges and confusion faced during such transitions. The task, then, is to reapply the developed strength and talents to the new situation. You reassert your feeling of growth by staying focused with the daily, weekly, and monthly religious practices that keep you close to the Lord when in between you are wholly engaged in things that appear and feel far from it. It is those who become distracted by the things of the world that misjudge their situation and are most susceptible to discouragement.

It isn't very different from moving to a new job or area or being released from a responsibility you love. You may sometimes find that the new situation requires you to make new friends or adjust to new working or social conditions. Perhaps acceptance is slow in coming or the overall circumstances are not as favorable as those in your previous location. This is the time to check your conditioning, spiritually hydrate, adjust your view of how to effectively apply your spiritual strengths, and move forward. It is not the time to look back and dwell on how good things were in the past. It is time to gather and refresh yourself with the Spirit and press forward, remaining steadfast (1 Corinthians 15:58; Hebrews 3:14).

The Savior Himself warned us of this danger when He said to those who desired to follow Him but were distracted by other things: "No man, having put his hand to the plough, and looking back, is fit for the kingdom of God" (Luke 9:62). Job's example and words after losing everything provide inspiration on the subject of faithful endurance. "Naked came I out of my mother's womb, and naked shall I return thither: the Lord gave, and the Lord hath taken away; blessed be the name of the Lord. . . . For I know that my redeemer liveth, and that he shall stand at the latter day upon the earth: And though after my skin worms destroy this body, yet in my flesh shall I see God. . . . I made a covenant. . . . Let me be weighed in an even balance, that God may know mine integrity" (Job 1:21; 19:25–26; 31:1, 6).

The way to avoid the downward pull of "spiritual vertigo" and the world is to press forward with steadfastness, seek out those who share your conviction, share each other's burdens, and then make sure you continue to stand on "good ground." By doing this, we cannot be dragged down. The counsel to us is clear, even at times of extreme tribulation: We can find protection by standing in holy places (Matthew 24:15).

NOTE

1. Personal conversations of the author with Allen C. Rozsa, 1975–77.

CHAPTER 12

Respecting the Trail

Riding in the mountains at 5,000 to 7,000 feet can be a beautiful experience. The combination of breathtaking views, smells that awaken the senses, and healthy exertion are hard to beat. The single track offers all of these and more. Respecting this beautiful environment is the foundation of preserving it for future experiences and generations. Nowadays, wherever we go, we encounter polluters, who seem to have little concern for anything other than themselves and their own gratification. They use the land and walk away seemingly unconcerned about how they might have left it for the next person or how they impact others who might be there at the same time.

On the trail there are a few who simply drop what they no longer need and move on. This can include litter of all types, dog or horse feces, and clothing. Some even deface the trail, which includes occasionally having an illegal campfire in the center of the trail, defacing trees, or riding out of control and repeatedly skidding tires, making deep furrows on the trail that in turn erode. Tire skidding is most damaging when the edge of the trail is torn apart, allowing erosion to eat into the trail itself. This, of course, is wholly avoidable by maintaining responsible speeds, communicating ahead, and understanding how to utilize both brakes and their individual touch to avoid unnecessary damage to the trail. The litter aspect is also avoidable by simply caring a bit more and accepting some responsibility for your actions.

While most of these activities seem like little things and must continue unabated over time to cause serious or permanent damage, a few can be quite devastating. Setting a campfire in an illegal location with thick foliage and overhanging trees is one of these. I have ridden in two different areas in Idaho after the ravages of a forest fire. The trail, of course, is still there, but the countryside will likely not be the same again during my lifetime. It is tragic, but once done, some damage cannot be easily undone.

Our lives are in many ways similar to a beautiful mountain path. Wear and tear occurs even with responsible usage, and some natural erosion is unavoidable, coming as the years pass. However, there are also ways a person can produce unnecessary or premature damage. I believe there are three basic ways to erode or pollute a life: through physical, spiritual, or prospects erosion.

Physical and spiritual erosion are connected. It does not matter which one leads; the other one soon follows. You cannot fill your mind with anger, wickedness, and perversion without it changing behavior, dress, and countenance. Likewise, you cannot damage and pollute your physical body without it changing attentiveness toward spiritual nourishment and dampening or destroying faith.

Paul asked the Corinthians, "Know ye not that your body is the temple of the Holy Ghost . . . ?" (1 Corinthians 6:19) and "Know ye not that ye are the temple of God, and that the Spirit of God dwelleth in you? If any man defile the temple of God, him shall God destroy; for the temple of God is holy, which temple ye are" (1 Corinthians 3:16–17).

John reminded us that the Holy Ghost's ability to dwell with us is dependent on our obedience (1 John 3:24). Paul put it all together most eloquently when he taught, "And what agreement hath the temple of God with idols? for ye are the temple of the living God; as God hath said, I will dwell in them, and walk in them; and I will be their God, and they shall be my people. Wherefore come out from among them, and be ye separate, saith the Lord, and touch not the unclean thing; and I will receive you" (2 Corinthians 6:16–17).

Our society today seems to have completely disregarded the concept that our bodies are sacred temples of God and the Holy Spirit. The concept that our physical body is a gift and was created in the image of God (Genesis 1:26–27; 9:6) is generally ignored in favor of the justification, "It's my body. I can do what I want with it." As a result, our physical bodies in many cases are polluted, abused, and more likely to be used as billboards or pin cushions than temples. Would you deface a sacred building with graffiti or punch random holes in the walls? The scriptures compare the human body to the most holy of Old Testament structures, the holy temple where God dwells. Both Moses and Solomon were given specific directions regarding the construction and use of the tabernacle and temple. It did not belong to them; it belonged to God. It was not to be used as a blank canvas upon which they could put any decoration desired. While such activities related to defacing our bodies with tattoos, intentional scarring, or multiple piercings pose some serious (but not life threatening) potential health problems,[1] they are more symptomatic of a lack of respect for one's temple. Unfortunately, such outward bodily disrespect is often associated with inward disrespect and pollution.

There is no serious difference of opinion regarding the damage, premature aging, and causes of death from internal bodily abuse caused by alcohol, tobacco, and drug usage. Statistics for 2006 causes of death indicate that the top five causes were, in order, heart attack, cancer, stroke, chronic lower respiratory (lung disease), and unintentional accidents (primarily vehicle related). These five causes accounted for two-thirds of all recorded deaths in 2006. The leading cause of death for those under the age of thirty-four remained historically consistent: unintentional accidents.[2] Which of these is not heavily associated with use or abuse of the referenced substances? None. People are the primary contributors to all these causes. To illustrate the point more effectively, let's examine smoking and its indirect effects on others. In 2006 the surgeon general issued a detailed report on the health consequences of involuntary exposure to tobacco smoke (referred to as secondhand smoke).[3] The conclusions were clear:

1. There is no risk-free level of exposure to secondhand smoke.
2. Secondhand smoke causes lung cancer.
3. Secondhand smoke causes heart disease.
4. Secondhand smoke causes acute respiratory effects.
5. Secondhand smoke can cause sudden infant death syndrome (SIDS) and other health consequences in infants and children.
6. Separating smokers from nonsmokers, cleaning the air, and ventilating buildings cannot eliminate secondhand smoke exposure.[4]

A further study published in April 2010 concluded that a combination of four unhealthy behaviors—smoking, lack of exercise, poor diet and substantial alcohol consumption increases the risk of premature death by twelve years.[5]

When we abuse our bodies, we not only lower our self-image, remove our access to the Holy Ghost, and distance ourselves from God, but we also destroy ourselves and damage countless others around us (see chapter 2).

The warning is clear: we cannot deface our personal temple internally or externally, spiritually or emotionally, and expect it to remain a temple in which the Holy Spirit can dwell. Some of these activities erode and pollute over time, while others can lead to rapid destruction, including spiritual and physical death.

Erosion of prospects results from the first two types of pollution. I have seen some high mountain trails that have lost their edge. Whole sections of the trail have eroded away, preventing future usage or making it extremely hazardous. Our futures can be marred or severely limited because of foolish behaviors performed without consideration for possible outcomes. Imagine how your future job prospects might be affected with a felony conviction on your record or as a result of brain damage or other physical limitations. It matters little if the permanent change in our prospects was unintended. Certainly too many have bought into the adversary's campaign that we can do anything now and the effects are far off, temporary, or maybe even minimal. The hard truth is that the enjoyment and satisfaction of life does not stop when you get older, and those who disregard their bodies risk the loss of much true joy along the way and valuable time at the end when their journey is unnecessarily cut short.

Consider also a shortsighted view toward education, particularly grades K–12, and how it might leave you wholly unprepared for the buffetings of the world. I spoke to a young man recently who attended the local high school. He, already at his young age, bore the scars of internal and external neglect and abuse of his temple. At the time, he was a junior and had decided not to make a serious effort at school. Although he was once an accomplished athlete, he was now excluded from competitive sports because of his poor attendance records, chronic tardiness, and low grades. His behavior was increasingly rebellious and selfish, and his attitude more negative each time I saw him. He had completely lost the light I once saw in his eyes, and his desire to achieve was gone. His response was that he already had an opportunity to earn decent money at a menial job as soon as he graduated, so good grades and further education were therefore unimportant.

I felt this was a far-reaching decision for a sixteen-year-old and that he couldn't possibly have made it with a clear view of its possible outcomes. I attempted to speak to him about his choices, and he was unwilling to consider a different point of view. The poor young man was severely limiting his options if his plan did not work out. Of course, he was unwilling to consider what it might be like to work in such an environment for the next forty years because he just wanted to be done with school. It's true that his perspective can change—and I pray that it does. But how many lost years and opportunities will it take before he figures it out and starts over?

Another type of prospect erosion is time on this earth. I loved my father dearly and would like nothing better than to have lunch with him today and discuss my work on this book and obtain his guidance. He was a wonderful and hard-working man. He was also honest and honorable but was not particularly religious until late in his life. While he made some courageous and righteous decisions the last ten years of his life, his was cut short by decisions he made during his teens through his forties. During his young years, he developed serious alcohol and smoking habits. He overcame both during his late forties because it was becoming threatening to both his job and his life, but the internal damage was already done. He passed away at the age of sixty-eight from complications with his lungs and cancer. The hidden curse in such behavior is that it not only takes you prematurely, but it limits and then destroys your life along the way. He was in and out of hospitals his last ten years, and from his forties on he was severely limited and could not engage in any mildly strenuous activity without gasping for air. He did much good during his life in all phases of his involvement, but he was robbed of much that he might have enjoyed, and all who loved him had their precious association with him cut short because of unwise choices that destroyed his earthly temple. He also missed important opportunities to grow spiritually and find true joy because of his long spiritual detour. Erosion of prospects, then, means lost opportunities in all areas over time because of shortsighted, unrighteous, and self-destructive behavior.

Many wonderful promises exist in the scriptures for those who respect the trail and their earthly temples. "They that wait upon the Lord shall renew their strength; they shall mount up with wings as eagles; they shall run, and not be weary; and they shall walk, and not faint" (Isaiah 40:31). Now that sounds like someone in good health.

Our Heavenly Father wants us to pass every test and overcome every obstacle. He gave us a spirit encased in a work of eternal fine art called a human body so that we might have success during this earth life in preparing ourselves to return to Him and also that we might experience meaningful joy and happiness along the path. The counsel we have received from Him and the revelatory guidance we continue to receive, if followed, will make that possible.

NOTES

1. "Tattoo Problems—Topic Overview," *WebMD*, (last updated September 4, 2008), http://webmd.com/skin-problems-and-treatments/tc/tattoo-problems-topic-overview.

2. Melonie Heron, PhD, Donna L. Hoyert, PhD, Sherry L. Murphy, BS, Jiaquan Xu, MD, Kenneth D. Kochanek, MA, and Betzaida Tejada-Vera, BS. "Deaths: Final Data for 2006," *National Vital Statistics Report* 57, no. 14 (April 17, 2009). http://www.cdc.gov/nchs/data/nvsr57/nvsr57_14.pdf.

3. Richard Carmona, MD, MPH, FACS, Surgeon General of the United States, "The Health Consequences of Involuntary Exposure to Tobacco Smoke," *A Report of the Surgeon General*, U.S.

Department of Health and Human Services (June 27, 2006), http://www.surgeongeneral.gov/library/secondhandsmoke/.

4. Ibid.

5. Elisabeth Kaavik, PhD, G. David Batty, PhD, Giske Ursin, MD, PhD, Rachel Huxley, DPhil, and Catharine R. Gale, PhD, "Influence of Individual and Combined Health Behaviors on Total and Cause-Specific Mortality in Men and Women," *Archives of Internal Medicine* 170, no. 8 (April 26, 2010): 711–18. http://archinte.ama-assn.org/cgi/content/short/170/8/711.

CHAPTER 13

Picking the Right Line

There are technical stretches along the path that require additional attention. These can be encumbered with rocks and roots or may involve slick wet hills, narrow bridges, loose gravel, or sand. Each of these requires adjustment. The most challenging are always easier if you pick a line through the stretch and predetermine how you will avoid the most troublesome spots as well as how you will hit the obstacles you cannot avoid.

There is a spot about 300 feet below the "pipeline" that presents such a problem. As you approach the spot coming uphill, there is a steep, smooth rise of about thirty feet, which culminates in a hump over a large root with a low-hanging branch. After the hump, there is a spot where the trail is split into two levels with about a foot between the levels. The lower level is good when coming down, but staying high helps keep momentum going up. Because the trail is split, each side of the path is only about six inches wide. The trail then curves sharply right (blind corner), and there is a wide crown of an exposed boulder on the right side that you must roll over. The lower part of the trail has roots that rob you of your momentum. The trail at that point is no longer split, and there is a 10- to 15-foot downward roll with a large root angled right to left across the trail. The top of this root is smooth from wearing, but it can be quite slick when wet and redirect your front wheel if not hopped or hit at greater than a forty-five degree angle. If your wheel is redirected, it is toward the drop-off, and you're in trouble.

After the root, you have about ten feet to pick up some momentum because there is a tree on the edge of the trail with a root system perpendicular to the trail running straight across. This requires a hop to get over the root, and the line is to the right toward the lesser thickness of the root system. Drifting to the left takes you into the trunk of the tree—also not good. As you can see, picking the proper line and sticking to it allows you to maintain momentum and overcome a succession of obstacles that come one after another. Getting off line at any point will likely prevent you from overcoming the next obstacle.

For many years, I have enjoyed snow skiing and have occasionally participated in or watched individuals run a tight slalom or downhill course. The momentum, strength, and rhythm necessary to successfully negotiate such a course are inspiring. Every competition has its moments when a skier catches an edge or gets off line for one reason or another and misses a gate. It simply is not possible to recover from such slight deviations at unforgiving speeds.

Our passage along life's path is similar in so many ways. It is best, of course, not to get off line in the first place. However, God provided a process, called repentance, which allows us to get back on track if it becomes necessary. One of the guiding principles we follow in my home is doing everything we can to "not make a mistake the first time." What does this mean? We recognize that commandments, covenants, virtuous standards, house rules, laws of the land, and so on are all obligations we must honor to keep our promises to the Lord. Setting a good example is one important reason we do this, but there is a deeper purpose.

We are grateful to Heavenly Father for our many blessings and feel we should always attempt to stand in "holy places" (Matthew 24:15). It has therefore been our family mantra that we do our best to keep the commandments every time. We recognize that once we compromise on one of these commandments or rules, it is *not* a rule, law, or a commandment to us anymore; it becomes a negotiation. This means that once we have crossed that particular line, we stand on the other side. As long as we stand there, we are faced with self-negotiation each time that particular rule or promise is tested to decide whether or not we will do it again.

No one can exist in this state for very long, for it is a slippery slope. Unchecked, it soon becomes less and less of a negotiation, then a habit, and finally an established part of our new behavior. The way back for a covenanting people is to repent and make or renew a covenant. This means we must take action to move back to "good ground" or a "holy place." This applies to house rules as well. The more we develop an attitude of compromising and negotiating on small things, the farther we get out of our planned line. We are disciplining ourselves in preparation for something. Why not make that something worthwhile? So in our family we have discovered that choosing to not miss church, scripture study, family prayers, service opportunities, family activities, or the opportunity to uplift another the first time is the key. Spiritual momentum is best maintained by not falling down the first time whenever possible.

Now, in spite of our collective and individual best efforts, we find ourselves falling down on occasion anyway. There is plenty of that in life without adding more ourselves. But the Lord said without hesitation, "I lay down my life for the sheep" (John 10:15). Our Savior willingly took upon Him our sins, pains, wounds at the hand of others, and all our other burdens (Matthew 8:17) and asks only that we do our best to accept His Atonement through the exercise of our faith by obedience and repentance. In doing this, we find peace, not confusion; healing, not pain; and a heart full of light rather than darkness.

It is miraculous that choosing the correct line to follow and sticking with it gives us not only spiritual elevation but also the strength to deal with other rules and laws, such as obeying the rules of your home, staying on top of homework, and honoring the commitments you have made to your team or coworkers. Such spiritual momentum also makes our travel along the narrow path seem easier; our burdens become lighter and our hopes become brighter.

There is one more critical component necessary to make this a successful process. Those in our respective flocks must be able to exercise their own right to choose, as they are able, and take title to these obligations themselves. For example, it is one thing for teenagers to tell their friends they cannot participate in certain activities on Sunday, watch an R-rated movie, or stay out past curfew because their parents won't let them. It is entirely different when a teenager tells his friends that he isn't going to watch an R-rated movie or stay out past curfew because he doesn't feel good about it himself. This position has conviction and commands respect from his peers because he is expressing his own feelings.

Certainly our interaction with children changes as they develop perspective and maturity and begin to more clearly understand right from wrong. Sometimes it seems like real parenting doesn't begin until children become more independent. There is no magical age that this happens, but as children mature, we begin to parent by consent out of respect and trust rather than because we are parents. My wife and I have realized that when we place our teenagers in the position that makes them the most responsible—that of exercising their own freedom to choose—they sometimes feel uncomfortable. When our teenagers are faced with a dilemma, we try to make it clear to them what the Lord's position is on the matter. We also clearly describe our position on that same matter and the choices that will put them on the right course. Then we pull the responsibility trigger—you know, the one that makes teenagers groan. We point out that they understand the Lord's and their parents' will, so they are now free to choose for themselves. One of our sons confessed recently that he would much rather have had us tell him what to do. Our responsibility as parents is to make sure our children have a clear understanding of what is right and why, and that we trust them to make a wise decision. When this method works, they are more likely to take title to the decision as their own.

This leaves one aspect unaddressed that has to do with spiritual gifts. Paul describes several of the gifts of the Spirit, or Holy Ghost (1 Corinthians 12:3–11; Hebrews 2:4). One particular gift mentioned is "differences of administrations" (1 Corinthians 12:5). This clearly applies to how each of us may approach our opportunities and obligations to serve God in accordance with His will. It also applies to how we manage, with Him, our individual lives. Knowing that "differences of administration" is a gift given to us to help us as we learn and grow is a critical advantage. Such understanding will aid us in managing our personal life, then our life with our spouse, then our life with children, and all the associated complexities, balances, and prioritization necessary along the way. This gift, like many of the others, can be received more abundantly ("according to His own will") as we grow in faithful experience (Hebrews 2:4).

One of my nephews had completed a successful and honorable two-year proselyting mission and was struggling with "spiritual vertigo" and readjustment. Neither of his parents had served in that way, and they asked me for input on how they could respond to his repeated comment that they didn't know what he was going through. I agreed to write him a letter because he could not make that particular argument in response to my counsel. I felt the Lord's inspiration in the response as I explained that, while he had just completed an important foundational experience in his life, such an experience was insufficient to teach him all that would be necessary in the next important step to manage the increasing complexity of life and continue to make progress. I counseled him that his religious leader and parents were his best resources because they have rich experience in this type of administration, which allowed them to have that gift more abundantly.

In this case, this extraordinary young man simply did not know how to manage school, athletics, and impending marriage. Of course he was on a steep learning curve, but Heavenly Father had surrounded him with wise and experienced stewards. Working with his parents and seeking and heeding their counsel, along with continued faithfulness and prayer, dissipated much of the trumpet's uncertain sound as he organized himself and prepared every needful thing (James 2:16; 1 Corinthians 14:8).

Like my nephew, we all learn, as we actively and seriously include the Lord in our travel along the path, that with time and necessity, the windows of Heaven open wider so that we might receive more abundantly the gifts of the Spirit. Until then, we are wise in learning from those who already have such gifts. We are told that as we seek earnestly, always remember for what these gifts are given, keep the commandments, and ask according to the will of God, that it will be done even as we ask (Matthew 7:7; 1 Corinthians 14:12).

It is therefore good to plan a line of progress, but it is better if we use the Lord's planned line and follow it by the guidance of the Holy Ghost. We learn the Lord's plan by study and prayer as well as from those the Lord has placed among us as our personal shepherds.

CHAPTER 14

The Downhill Ride

My typical morning ride takes me to Big Rock. Less often will I continue on to Rudy's Flats. The round trip to Big Rock will take a reasonably strong rider less than an hour, excluding any rest time. Much has been discussed in earlier chapters about the ride. Here we will discuss the payoff for any out and back rider—the ride down. I love the ride down, especially on a warm day. As sweat from the ride up cools your body and as the rhythm and undulations of the trail pull you in, it is possible to feel that both you and the bike become connected with the track.

Heading down the trail is not all fun and games. It has its own set of requirements to have a positive experience. Posture and center of gravity must be adjusted, which is done by sliding your body back on the seat a few inches while rising slightly on the seat so you can take any bumps more smoothly. This is important even with full suspension. Sliding back allows your center of gravity to be slightly farther back over your rear tire, which will help avoid the previously discussed over-the-handlebars flight.

The next set of rules has to do with arms and hands. It is not usually legs or cardio conditioning that requires frequent stops with the less experienced downhill rider. It is the conditioning and strength of the arms, wrists, and hands. The ride down is where this is most evident. A consistent, firm grip on the handlebars is critical, or a bump can dislodge the hands, almost always causing an accident. Carefully focusing ahead on the trail and picking a good line help, but there are still those moments when a patch of shade hiding a protruding rock or momentum carrying you into a root or loose gravel can cause unexpected problems. Intense hand and forearm isometrics are involved for seventeen to twenty-five minutes from Big Rock down—longer if you start higher. It is difficult to get that part of your body in shape for this, especially if you are already fatigued from thirty to fifty minutes of uphill riding.

Simply gripping the handlebars is not sufficient; the rider must also constantly be working the brakes. The back brake is the most useful, but careful usage of the front brake helps. Front brake usage must be practiced because improper pressure will lock the front tire and land you on your helmet quicker than anything else. The result is a pair of uninitiated hands that are too fatigued to grip the latch to open the car door when arriving at the bottom of the hill. I remember one particularly difficult ride on Adam's Gulch Loop Trail in Sun Valley, Idaho. Some of the riders had such difficulty with their hands and wrists that it was days before they were able to use them normally again. Wet conditions and damp brakes only make things worse.

Inattentiveness can produce the same results. I was headed down one day and pulled over to the side of the trail to wait for some hikers to pass. I noticed up ahead a young man with headphones. He was singing at the top of his lungs and whipping his head around with one hand on the handlebars of his bike while the other held an MP3 player in the air. He was showboating a bit as he rode past some girl hikers. I thought of the stretch of roots and rocks that were around the corner ahead of him about a hundred feet distant. He disappeared around the corner, and before I got going again, I heard a loud cry from that direction. Yes, you guessed it—he had hit the rocky area and took a hard spill. By the time I passed him, he was standing again, brushing off the dirt and talking to himself about where the rocks had come from.

After years of riding, your hands and forearms strengthen and the isometrics are not noticeable. An experienced guide must carefully watch over his group to make sure they are having no difficulty on the downward trip. A few years ago on a family vacation, one of my older teenage nephews and my twenty-something-year-old son were having arm wrestling contests. I was in my early fifties at the time, and they goaded me into a test. The two were weight lifters, football players, and in top condition. After defeating them three out of four times right and left handed, one asked me the secret of my arm wrestling prowess. I responded that it was years of gripping the handlebars and brakes while biking. They looked at me with skepticism, and to this day I think they consider it a fluke. The truth is that it takes tremendous development of hands, wrists, and forearms to comfortably negotiate an uninterrupted trip down the mountain trail.

The last area I wish to address here is downhill courtesy. During the euphoria of a downhill run, it is easy to forget it is not a racecourse and that you worked hard to get up the hill. The International Mountain Biking Association (IMBA) has six well established rules for mountain riding. Rule number four is "Yield Appropriately."[1] It briefly references many of the concepts discussed in previous chapters and also includes the counsel that downhill riders should always yield to those going uphill. It further advises that we should strive to make each pass safe. On the Mueller Park Trail, this means that the downhill rider needs to communicate ahead and always be able to pull over and step with his bike to the side of the trail so the upward traveler can easily move past. Yes, the golden rule is a written part of mountain biking. Those who get lost in their own selfish ride down at least inconvenience others and at worst risk serious accidents and injury.

As we move through life, there are times when we struggle and other times when our passage seems surprisingly easy. Of course we could not appreciate the good times without the periods of adversity. Such conditions are integral to both our individual plan of happiness and our personal salvation. Peter understood the importance of opposition and trial in this life: "That the trial of your faith, being much more precious than of gold that perisheth, though it be tried with fire, might be found unto praise and honor and glory at the appearing of Jesus Christ: Whom having not seen, ye love; in whom, though now ye see him not, yet believing, ye rejoice with joy unspeakable and full of glory: Receiving the end of your faith, even the salvation of your souls" (1 Peter 1:7–9).

As we understand and place in proper perspective both our trials and our blessings, we can more clearly see the necessary eternal balance that alternatively strengthens us and then tests that strength. Making correct choices moves us forward and upward, ever deepening our roots and enriching our soil as we develop the characteristics of Christ. The result is that we become so much more than we otherwise would have been. This, then, is the essence of our journey along the narrow passage of life. We see the culmination of this in the parable of the ten virgins found in the Gospel of Matthew (Matthew 25:1–13).

In reference to the Second Coming of the Lord (the Bridegroom), the parable states that the "kingdom of heaven be likened unto ten virgins which took their lamps, and went forth to meet the bridegroom. And five of them were wise, and five were foolish" (Matthew 25:1–2). Who are the virgins? They are believers, or they would not have been invited to meet the bridegroom. Each of them accepted the invitation, yet five, even though they clearly believed, were insufficiently prepared, or as John would say, "lukewarm" (Revelation 3:15–16).

What is the difference between the wise and foolish virgins in the parable? It is not the amount of oil in their lamps, for each virgin had a full lamp of oil at the start. It was the fact that the wise virgins carried with them additional vessels of oil to refill their lamps when they burned low—"oil in their vessels with their lamps"—and the foolish virgins "took no oil with them" (Matthew 25:1–13). The tragic result for the foolish virgins was that as the evening wore on and the oil in the lamps was consumed, their lamps burned low or went out. The wise virgins refilled their lamps but had not enough for the others. The foolish virgins ran to buy additional oil and missed the coming of the Bridegroom. The scene at the closed door is heartbreaking as the five believing but foolish virgins returned to find "the door was shut." The message is brought home in the Bridegroom's answer to the foolish virgins' plea, "saying, Lord, Lord, open to us. But he answered and said, Verily I say unto you, I know you not. Watch therefore, for ye know neither the day nor the hour wherein the Son of man cometh" (Matthew 25:11–13).

The oil referred to in the parable is symbolic of something that we become through a life of obedience and service and the development of a willing mind and heart. It cannot be shared; it must grow within you through regular daily and weekly practices and a life of careful spiritual nourishment. The understanding developed through prayer and study that is put to work every day makes it so. The question is not, "What do you have?" Rather, it is, "Who have you become?" It is not how you have developed and adorned your outward appearance or position in the community; it is the nature of your heart and the pure love of Christ you have developed in your soul. It is to these the Lord speaks when He says, "Come unto me, all ye that labor and are heavy laden, and I will give you rest. Take my yoke upon you, and learn of me; for I am meek and lowly in heart: and ye shall find rest unto your souls" (Matthew 11:28–29).

NOTE

1. International Mountain Biking Association, "Rules of the Trail," www. imba.com/about/rules_trail.

CHAPTER 15

Why Me?

Please forgive me as a wince of pain or sigh of frustration escapes my lips each time I read this chapter. "Why me?" is a question that is only asked when you find it hard to believe what just happened. Some of the experiences related here and in other places in this book recall feelings that are not pleasant to remember. There are two types of experiences on the Mueller Park Trail that evoke such reactions. They fall into the category of accidents and mechanical problems. Both tend to seriously diminish one's enjoyment.

Mechanical problems can occur at any time, even if you keep your bike tuned properly. These problems tend to occur when you are stressing the bike as well as your body, say up a hill or through a rock field. One morning early in the season, as I stood on my pedals to push up one of the two steep climbs at the beginning of the ride, my chain snapped. This was not at the expansion link but the main part of the chain. This is a turn-around-and-take-your-bike-to-the-shop moment. I have had the expansion link break, which can be managed if you have the right parts, but it is also not fun and many riders do not carry extra expansion links. On another occasion, my rear brake cable or shifting cable has snapped, which didn't end the ride immediately but seriously changed the downhill experience because you can't use the front brake too aggressively without flipping the bike. I also remember my rear shifting cable snapping one morning on the early climbs as well. There are few things as uncomfortable as your gears suddenly shifting to their hardest setting while straining up a steep incline.

Sometimes other mechanical problems do not end your ride but make particularly the uphill portion frustrating. These tend to be times when the chain has become stretched or the shifting mechanism is out of tune, and certain gears may pop out or the chain may jump or slip. You ask, "Why me?" because this usually happens when you are peddling up a slope and need the extra momentum the most. The slippage can cause such disruption that a person can end up off the bike and on the ground. Some of these "why me?" moments can even be self-inflicted. When riding another's bike on an unfamiliar trail, I reached the top and my thighs were completely worn down to jelly. Upon closer inspection, I discovered the seat was set an inch or two inches too low, something I should have noticed earlier but overlooked. With the seat low, it kept me from extending my legs and using the full range of muscles. The effort was therefore limited to my thighs, producing poor performance and big-time thigh muscle fatigue. Not fun.

The other kind of problem can be caused by a freak circumstance or combination of unexpected events that produce an accident. Some are completely unavoidable, and others certainly could have been avoided. One unavoidable situation happened to me about ten years ago, and I still watch carefully whenever I pass the spot. Just above the "pipeline" is a transition from uphill riding to some mostly downhill or level riding. It starts with a steep downhill right curve. I always call out to make sure other riders are aware around the blind corner. On this day there were no other riders, so I came around the corner and picked up speed for a brief uphill climb before some nice level rolling. But I was unaware of a hazard near the ground. There was a thick, leafless branch that was sticking out onto the trail just off the ground, and it became lodged in my front spokes and immediately stopped the rotation of my tire. I was traveling at a good rate, so I did what must have been a beautiful front summersault in near pike position and hit the ground squarely on my head and upper back. I lay there for a minute or two taking a physical inventory and wondering, "Why me?" I was certainly not the first one on the trail that morning. Perhaps a dozen or more riders had passed that spot. But the branch position was perfect for my tire at that moment. I looked back at my bike and saw the front rim was bent as well. I took my tire off and pounded it so the wheel would at least turn, but I couldn't get it to the point that it could be ridden. Oh, there's nothing like an extra forty-five-minute walk down the trail to make your day.

Was I blessed in these situations? Yes, because I was not seriously injured. Was the enjoyment of the ride that day ruined or severely diminished? Of course it was. Could similar experiences have ended in serious injury or death? Yes, this has happened to others on the trail. As we pass through life, we experience these moments in different ways. There are opportunities along the way to complain, murmur, and even curse God should we be of a mind to do so. They can be particularly difficult if we feel we have been following the Lord's plan and trying to do all we can to obey His will. We may be solidly on the narrow path and still experience terrible trials.

We pass through life, sometimes for long periods, without a serious challenge or setback. We fall into a daily routine that takes on a feeling of "sameness" and lulls us into a belief that every day in the future will repeat the established pattern. This can go on for years. Of course, there are bumps in the road. But like mountain biking, they jar us and then pass, and we fall back into our rhythm again and hardly remember. There is little or no indication that a day-changing or life-changing event is just around the corner. Then one day we awaken and realize that life will never be the same again because of the passing of a loved one, a serious illness or injury, financial disruption, a natural disaster, a child who wanders on strange paths, new and unexpected demands on our time, or a dramatic change in home or family circumstances.

The book of Ruth tells us of a woman named Naomi who traveled with her husband and two sons to the land of Moab. This displacement occurred because of a famine in their homeland of Judah. While in this strange land, Naomi's husband died. This was, of course, a difficult time, but she had her two sons who took wives of the women of Moab and together cared for their mother. After a passage of time, both of Naomi's sons died, leaving the three women alone. Naomi, a kind and loving mother-in-law, released her daughters-in-law from any obligation and determined to return to her people in Judah. Ruth chose to stay with Naomi (Ruth 1:1–14).

Naomi attempted to talk Ruth out of it by explaining her poor prospect of finding a husband in a strange land with no kinfolk and different beliefs. However, Ruth would not hear of it. Her response contains no "why me." "And Ruth said, Intreat me not to leave thee, or to return from following after thee: for whither thou goest, I will go; and where thou lodgest, I will lodge: thy people shall be my people, and thy God my God: Where thou diest, will I die, and there will I be buried: the Lord do so to me, and more also, if ought but death part thee and me." When Naomi saw that Ruth was "steadfastly minded to go with her, then she left speaking unto her" (Ruth 1:16–18). Of course the rest of the story is that Ruth was blessed for her faithfulness, eventually married into the line of Judah, and through her direct lineage was born King David (Ruth 4:17).

So what did Ruth do? Her reaction is not only inspiring but instructive. First, she was not consumed with self-victimization upon the loss of her husband. Then she demonstrated her willingness to be selfless by putting Naomi's well-being first. Ruth followed faithfully without murmur or complaint. Here is a woman that was by all outward appearances ordinary. She had different beliefs and was going to a strange land in a situation where by tradition her prospects for a better life as a widow were bleak. Yet, she went without question or hesitation, in spite of resistance from Naomi. Would it have been understandable if Ruth had cursed her situation, complained to God, or returned to the safety of life with her kinsmen? Of course, but she demonstrated that rare and wonderful quality found in all the great and faithful leaders of scripture. She had faith in God and an unflinching willingness to follow His will even if expressed indirectly through others. When presenting herself before Boaz, she was told by Naomi to follow some specific instructions. And what was her answer? "All that thou sayest unto me I will do" (Ruth 3:5).

Herein we find a plain example for how to deal with the great trials in our life. In contrast, the children of Israel and their constant murmuring to Moses make plain to us what not to do. Faithful disciples pray for protection, guidance, inspiration, and prosperity. Certainly many would be justified in receiving such. But life does not always go that smoothly. Famine sometimes strikes us, we are sometimes commanded to do things that are difficult or seem impossible, and sometimes we find ourselves in situations where we cannot figure out how to even begin tackling the problem. Imagine Moses when he was first commanded to lead his people out of bondage. He had already been exiled from Egypt and was essentially a nomad in the wilderness. He was slow of speech and believed himself to be a "nobody" (Exodus 3:11, 13; 4:1, 10). Yet, he obeyed, trusted in the Lord, and went about his duty.

Moses received earthly deliverance, but not all of us do. Stephen was not delivered from those who wished to stone him (Acts 7:54–60). Abel was not delivered from Cain (Genesis 4:8). Jonathan was not delivered from death on Mount Gilboa (2 Samuel 1:21–23). John the Baptist was not delivered from Herod (Mark 6:27). Neither were many of the early apostles, including Paul, James, and Peter, delivered from their fates. So what can we learn from these apparent contradictions?

Trials that seem contrary to our righteous prayers and efforts do not necessarily mean we are doing something wrong. We are here on this earth to have a collection of growth experiences, to face opposition and temptation and through it develop and exercise faith and make correct choices that move us closer to God. This cannot happen if our life is completely devoid of any challenge or trial. It is the very nature of this earth life that allows us to have those days that make us wonder, "Why me?" or, "Why now, just when things were going so well?" or, "Why now, when things are so difficult?" The answer is that God has a plan designed to refine and develop us spiritually into persons that will be worthy to dwell with Him and our Savior and do the eternal work They have prepared for the faithful. Refinement is uncomfortable. Preparation takes action and time. But the path is clear. The Savior Himself commanded us, "Enter ye in at the strait gate: for wide is the gate, and broad is the way, that leadeth to destruction, and many there be which go in thereat: Because strait is the gate, and narrow is the way, which leadeth unto life, and few there be that find it" (Matthew 7:13–14).

At times each of us is driven to our knees with seemingly overwhelming burdens or with sorrow that comes from deep within our heart. These days can bring us to the edge of a deep abyss where we cry out for help and feel we cannot take another step and would that we could let this cup pass from our lips. These are times when we speak in the midst of unbearable sorrow and our Father knows that we would consent to being taken if it were His will. Moses had one of these days when the children of Israel tormented him because they were tired of manna and demanded meat. He cried to the Lord, "I am not able to bear all this people alone, because it is too heavy for me. And if thou deal thus with me, kill me, I pray thee, out of hand, if I have found favor in thy sight; and let me not see my wretchedness" (Numbers 11:14–15). Our spirits may be racked with responsibilities we feel we cannot bear, with torment, with sorrow, with physical or spiritual pain, or with fear as we question if there is any hope at all. There are days when we cannot at the beginning see how we will survive to the evening. A loving Heavenly Father has not left us alone, for He promises to give "power to the faint; and to them that have no might he increaseth strength" (Isaiah 40:29).

The cause of that moment when our spirit reaches its breaking point isn't as important as what we do with it. For it is in those moments that we can also feel the spirit of the Lord's love wash over us like cool waters on a hot day. The calming comes, the trembling stops; then we hear the words of our Savior and friend: "Love one another, as I have loved you. Greater love hath no man than this, that a man lay down his life for his friends. Ye are my friends" (John 15:12–14). In these quiet moments, we may understand some small portion of the Savior's feelings as He prayed that the cup could pass from His lips (Matthew 26:39; Mark 14:36; Luke 22:42). But then in the crowning submission of all history, He said, "Nevertheless not as I will, but as thou wilt" (Matthew 26:39; see Mark 14:36 and Luke 22:42).

He is our friend. He loves us, and He laid down His life for us for a purpose—that we might overcome our challenges and return and be with Him again. These are times when we come to know God and feel Christ's unconditional love for us. As we are encircled by the Spirit, we understand that we are not forgotten. We have a reason for being. We have value beyond measure, and we have never been alone.

CHAPTER 16

It's a Beautiful Day
for a Ride

It's 6:30 on a Saturday morning in July, and all is quiet as I roll out of bed. I step out the front door to get a sense of the temperature and weather. Quietly I put on my riding clothes, grab my helmet and sunglasses, and give my sweetheart a kiss on the cheek. She knows I will be back by about 8:15, ready to get going with the regular responsibilities we have planned for the day. After checking air pressure, drinking some water, and filling my water bottle with ice and water, I'm on my way up to the trailhead. The morning is still cool, but I know that it will become much warmer as the sun rises. I do one more check of my brakes, lock my rear shock, stretch a bit, and ride the short distance to the trailhead from my car to loosen up. At the trailhead there are, as usual, about a dozen cars that have already disgorged their occupants. The cars sit patiently, awaiting their masters' return.

It is clear some bikers and walkers are already on the hill, so I take a mental note to make sure I call out my approach on the blind corners. After a few more moments of stretching—I find I need that more with age—and setting my bike meter and timer, off I go. I cross the bridge and gather momentum for the first two climbs, standing up as I approach them. It goes smoothly, and I stay in the gears I had planned. The ride continues to rise through the first two sharp switchbacks and then around what I call big bend, which is another stand-up pedal stretch. I approach the first outlook and am about one-third of the way to Big Rock. I have passed a couple of walkers on their way up, and an early-bird biker or two have come by on their way down. The downhill bikers don't call out, but luckily I come upon them on one of the straight stretches, so there are no problems. I notice fresh, slightly deeper tire tracks in the dust, which indicates bikers are not too far ahead of me going up. I use it for motivation to keep my pace up and try to catch them.

I approach the first inside curve and gain a little bit of downhill momentum for the first time in the ride and then hit another long outside climb to a series of four small rises I call the roller coaster coming down. Visibility is good here to the second inside turn and the halfway mark (in time) of the ride. I'm at about eighteen minutes, which is pretty good for me nowadays, although when I rode the trail more often eight years ago, I would reach this point in two to three fewer minutes. Another outside uphill climb and two more beautiful scenic view spots before I head for the last inside turn before the "pipeline." The climb from the third inside turn to the pipeline is some of the most technical on the trail and includes split levels, some more steep stretches, and a final uphill section through a rock field that requires momentum and a proper line to negotiate without touching. I do not like to touch down. It means momentum is gone, and with some of my riding buddies, you lose credibility points. I stand up on this stretch as well and am reminded how much easier it is to manage my balance while standing and pedaling. I make it around the outside curve to the pipeline and find a group of bikers resting and enjoying the view. Many stop here to catch their breath after the tough stretch, but I continue on, knowing that after one more brief uphill push there is a nice portion of downward rolling.

The first downward roll is around a sharp blind corner. Every year, riders approach this too quickly or without calling out, and there are accidents or places where they skid off the trail, eating away at the trail width right at the critical corner stretch. It is about a foot wide here now because there are already spots where bikers have torn away parts of the trail by skidding out of control. I call out and gain momentum for a good uphill stretch to the next inside turn. It was at this point five years ago that I surprised a juvenile moose in the spring. It was as large as a horse and trotted ahead of me on the trail until the next inside turn and then lumbered up into the trees without looking back. The trail now is fast, rolling, and relatively level, except for one little uphill area that can become gluey mud if it has rained. The key in this thirty-foot stretch is to keep your momentum and not have to pedal so hard that you spin your tires. This avoids a messy dismount and walk to a dry spot. It is dry today, so I stand and pedal up through the trees, calling out again for the next turn. The outside turn here is heavy with foliage on both sides, which masks a steep drop-off to the left and requires calling out frequently due to restricted sight.

I cross a short bridge and approach the first long, wide bridge on the trail. It is a beautiful spot where walkers with dogs often stop so their dogs can be refreshed. It is the first water since the trailhead, about thirty minutes into the ride. The approaches to both ends of the bridge were rebuilt about sixteen years ago by my son Travis and his friend Reggie for the friend's Eagle Scout project and remain in pretty good condition. It took them many hours to haul the railroad ties to this location for the work to repair the approaches. I think about it every time I cross this bridge.

After the bridge, there is a steep and always wet uphill push and then another narrower bridge that requires a six to eight-inch hop to get onto. The bridge is so narrow that if you lose your balance, it is likely you will end up lying sidewise in the marshy creek that runs under it. I build momentum and stand up for the hop with no problem (there is a rock just before the bridge that helps you ramp up right onto the higher level if you hit it just right). The trail then winds to another outside turn and more relatively level riding. I pass the flat-sided rock and notice it is still there to remind me that I should remain aware and focused now that I am approaching the end of the uphill ride to Big Rock, and I am feeling fatigued.

There are very steep, long drop-offs to the left all along the trail here and some slick, flat-angled rocks to cross. Keeping balance and focusing ahead are important in this stretch. There is a slight incline, a blind right turn, and a fifty- to sixty-foot narrow bridge that cannot accommodate passing. A huge porcupine that lives under or near this bridge is occasionally on the trail in this area. I approach and cross the last inside turn, which also has a bridge crossing a small stream. The trail then climbs again to a steep outside turn that has another rock field. I pick my usual outside line, stand up, and pump to get around the rocky bend, calling ahead and preparing for a difficult hop over a large tree root across the trail complicated by a rock on the right side. This spot is only about four inches wide and allows no margin for error. The hop must be just right or you get another dismount and little walk. After surmounting the last material obstacle, it's a gradual uphill climb for another two hundred feet or so to Big Rock, and I'm done. I coast my bike around the corner and lay it down near the bench where several travelers already sit.

A curved root lies to the side that I love to sit down on,

and I do so after stretching my hamstrings and calves out a bit. I will often call my sweetheart, if it is not too early, and tell her I made it safely to the rock one more time and when to expect me home. A few mornings I will call to harass one of my riding buddies about sleeping in instead of coming up the hill. Some pleasant conversation with other morning travelers, some water, and a beautiful view make the morning fantastic. And it's not yet 7:30 a.m. I mount my bike, unlock the rear shock (I prefer to hard tail it up the hill), and head down, keeping a reasonable speed so as to avoid inconveniencing those coming up. A few walkers and a rider have unleashed dogs that cause some problems for other trail users, but I dismount and allow them to pass by. Many more are on the trail on the lower stretches, and by the time I get to the trailhead, even more are getting started. (Many who use the trail seem to arrive between 8:00 and 8:30 a.m. on these days.)

My ride completed, I load the bike back into my car, check for any new scrapes or damage (I notice a new cut on my shin from a branch on the way down), and drive home. Another beautiful day has started with a great experience. I overlook the strain and challenge of the ride and focus on the feeling of accomplishment, the exercise, and the enjoyment.

Our daily experience away from the mountain can be the same. Each day can be a mixed bag of challenges, tasks, disappointments, and accomplishments. By focusing on our overall progress, staying close to our spiritual guides, engaging in daily nourishment, and learning to love those with whom we are traveling during the exceptional adventure that this life truly is, we can find inner strength, rest, peace, and joy, no matter what each day brings. My rides up the mountain remind me of this and how blessed I am not just to be able to sit on the bench at Big Rock one more time, but also to share the accomplishments of each day with a loving Father in Heaven, a wonderful companion, and a family that makes every step along the way worthwhile.

How to Recognize
a Mountain Biker

Whether planning to travel along the narrow path
or a mountain single track, it is important to
have an experienced guide, as discussed in chapter 4. Choosing proper earthly trail guides is important.
How do we identify them? Some assistance can again be
provided by our comparison to mountain biking. It is difficult to identify a quality guide if all you plan to do is stand
in the middle of the sidewalk and watch people pass by. You
can get some indication from their outward appearance, of
course, but less obvious indications tell the real story.

One sure way to tell an experienced mountain biker is
to look at his shins and the back and side of his calves. Why?

As you can tell from many of the experiences included in this book, there are times during almost every ride when you need to dismount quickly. With any quick mount or dismount, the pedals or sprocket will likely catch the front or back of your legs. This usually leaves sprocket-shaped grease marks, scrapes or scratches, cuts, and by the end of the season, telltale scars. I say this a bit tongue-in-cheek, but any experienced rider can relate. This also leads us to a more important eternal principle that I believe makes an excellent conclusion for this guide for spiritual growth.

No question, this earth is a battleground. A war has been waged for the souls of men since the dim reaches of our existence prior to this life. Satan is the leader of the opposition. His forces are organized, relentless, and always awake and working. We, who overcame the rebellion of Satan and kept the first estate (Jude 1:6), earned the right to come to this earth to gain bodily temples and develop faith. Although we are Satan's targets, there are forces for righteousness on our side. Those forces include our Heavenly Father, Jesus Christ, angelic hosts commissioned to minister and protect mankind, the writings of prophets and inspired individuals long passed on, individuals among us who are called to specific prophetic assignments, and others who are called by the Spirit into our path. God works His marvelous work and wonder (Isaiah 29:14) through all these resources and more. Righteous forces will ultimately triumph, but we cannot even begin to imagine the cost in human souls, pain, suffering, and personal loss.

One thing that can be said with certainty is that none of us will pass this way unscathed. Many of the prophets have suffered mightily in the wilderness or during trials. Joseph suffered unjustly at the hand of his brothers (Genesis 37:28) and at the hand of Potiphar (Genesis 39:20). Even though the end of Joseph's story was a happy one and clearly the process and result were God's plan to preserve the family of Jacob for great things, Joseph surely suffered mightily along the way.

We too can become injured and faint from the battles we are called to fight. We have been given the armor of God to protect us if we choose to strap it on and keep it clean and pure (Ephesians 6:10–18). Properly chosen guides can help keep our armor in pristine condition and teach us how to use it wisely. Clearly Joseph was taught obedience, hard work, and trust by his parents and God. These qualities were refined by the fires of great trial. Such qualities are found in not only the great scriptural leaders and prophets but also all those who serve as God commanded Solomon, "And thou, Solomon my son, know thou the God of thy father, and serve him with a perfect heart and with a willing mind: for the Lord searcheth all hearts, and understandeth all the imaginations of the thoughts: if thou seek him, he will be found of thee; but if thou forsake him, he will cast thee off for ever" (1 Chronicles 28:9). These are the people to whom the Lord has said, "Ask, and it shall be given you; seek, and ye shall find; knock, and it shall be opened unto you: For every one that asketh receiveth; and he that seeketh findeth; and to him that knocketh it shall be opened" (Matthew 7:7–8). But they do not stand alone. Each one of us has been given that same promise by the Savior himself.

There is one other quality that Ruth shared with great men like Abraham, Moses, Joseph, Peter, Paul, and others. These individuals recognized the same principle taught by Theodore Roosevelt at the Paris Sorbonne University one hundred years ago. One brief portion of his address makes the point precisely:

> It is not the critic who counts; not the man who points out how the strong man stumbles, or where the doer of deeds could have done them better. The credit belongs to the man who is actually in the arena, whose face is marred by dust and sweat and blood; who strives valiantly; who errs, who comes short again and again, . . . who knows great enthusiasms, the great

devotions; who spends himself in a worthy cause; who at the best knows . . . the triumph of high achievement, and who at the worst, if he fails, at least fails while daring greatly, so that his place shall never be with those cold and timid souls who neither know victory nor defeat.[1]

Contemplating this statement provides thoughtful insight into who we really are and where we need to stand. It reinforces that there are three kinds of people in the world today. The first two types we find on the arena floor, some motivated by righteous goals and others striving for selfish, hateful, and wicked results. These two groups are engaging in the fight that will make a difference for others in the world, either for good or for evil. They are doing all they can to make that difference. They know where they are and are taking action. The third group includes all those sitting in the bleachers. They cheer, they critique, and they observe and occasionally move around to get a better seat closer to the action or move farther away. These are the critics. They may know all the key statistics of those in the arena, but they do not make a difference; they do not act. Their eternal situation is determined by their own inaction and by the action of others on the floor of the arena.

Yet, many in this third group sincerely believe that by observing they are accomplishing something, when they are not. Some even campaign in their own self-important belief that others should follow them to their special seating area in the stands. It is an effective tool of the adversary to convince them that they are doing something when they are not, that they have enough oil when they do not, or that they are sufficiently prepared when there is much still to do. He tells them a little distraction does not hurt, that a little lie or taking advantage of others can be justified, and that in the end everything will be okay because they didn't do anything seriously wrong. Yet those who spend their lives in entertainment and distraction never become what they could be, and in eternity they will find themselves falling far short: "I know thy works, that thou art neither cold nor hot: I would thou wert cold or hot. So then because thou art lukewarm, and neither cold nor hot, I will spue thee out of my mouth" (Revelation 3:15–16).

We are not only commanded to "obey" and "refrain from," but more important, we are also commanded to "do" (James 1:22) many good and worthwhile things to help to bring to pass God's work. And what is God's great love and work? "For God so loved the world, that he gave his only begotten Son, that whosoever believeth in him should not perish, but have everlasting life. For God sent not his Son into the world to condemn the world; but that the world through him might be saved" (John 3:16–17). In these verses, Jesus tells us of the great work that is His and Heavenly Father's: that we might "have everlasting life," that His Father—our Father—loved each of us so much that He created a plan that would allow us to live and grow here on earth and repent and overcome our mistakes and return to Him. This plan required His Son, even our Savior Jesus Christ, as a sacrifice to pay the price for our mistakes, transgressions, and sins. This is the greatest demonstration of that godly love and witnesses beyond question the importance of such work to God. We are His work!

This requires those who count themselves as sincere believers to be in the arena fighting the good fight. It is imperative that each person be absolutely positive that they are fighting on God's side because Satan is a master at deception and is able to mislead even those who see themselves as devout (Matthew 24:24). It is not necessary for us to be the greatest warriors in the fight, but it is necessary that we give all we have and do all we can. Yes, those of us on the arena floor will stumble; we will be wounded time and again, experience loss of blood, and even be dislocated from our planned line of travel once in a while. But we will be fighting valiantly, and we will not be alone. That is what is meant when the psalmist tells us, "Yea, though I walk through the valley of the shadow of death, I will fear no evil: for thou art with me; thy rod and thy staff they comfort me" (Psalm 23:4).

It is this effort to diligently understand the Lord's will and then do it, even though we may fear and tremble at times, that is at the very heart of becoming the kind of person that will come unto Him. As a good mountain biker is able to achieve the desired results by following basic principles, so also can we as we travel along life's narrow path. The result is worth it, as promised by the psalmist: "The Lord is my shepherd; I shall not want. He maketh me to lie down in green pastures: he leadeth me beside the still waters. He restoreth my soul: he leadeth me in the paths of righteousness. . . . Thou anointest my head with oil; my cup runneth over. Surely goodness and mercy shall follow me all the days of my life: and I will dwell in the house of the Lord for ever" (Psalm 23:1–6).

This, my friends, is worth the fight. Come, let us make these principles part of our souls and ride together with a worthy guide.

NOTE

1. Theodore Roosevelt, "The Man in the Arena," address delivered to the Paris, Sorbonne University, April 23, 1910. *Almanac of Theodore Roosevelt*, http://www.theodore-roosevelt.com /trsorbonnespeech.html.

DISCUSSION QUESTIONS

1. Why is mountain biking such an excellent vehicle for teaching gospel principles?

2. Why is it important to understand where and who we are in relation to God?

3. What is our spiritual objective and what kind of person do we need to become to get there?

4. How do we continue to parent as our children become more independent?

5. Is there a method for empowering spiritual growth?

6. Why do we sometimes feel like we are in spiritual freefall when we are doing the right things?

7. How can we more effectively deal with adversity?

8. How do we recognize when we are on the sidelines versus on the trail?

9. How can we overcome offense and avoid its bedfellows, anger, bitterness, and hate?

10. Where do we find, and how do we follow, the map we need so we can see the big picture in life?

11. How can we effectively shepherd others?

12. Why is momentum so important it's almost like cheating in life?

13. Why is it so important to pick our guides carefully and then follow them?

14. When is the harder road the easier road?

15. Why can Satan's plan to give us "nothing" be so appealing?

16. Does prayer have real power, and how can it make a difference?

17. In what way can a sense of humor keep you on the right path?

18. What subtle attacks drain our spiritual energy?

19. How can we be fortified to withstand any challenge or attack?

ABOUT THE AUTHOR

CLARK R. BURBIDGE was born and raised in the high mountain valleys of the Rockies. He received a BS in finance from the University of Utah and an MBA from the University of Southern California. He spent the past thirty-one years working in banking, project finance, investment banking, and more recently as a chief financial officer for three different companies. His career has taken him throughout the nation and world.

He has been actively involved in community and church service, including lay youth and adult ministry for over thirty-five years. He continues to enjoy swimming, scuba diving, mountain/road biking, history, composing and playing instrumental music, writing, and anything in which his children are involved.

Clark and his sweetheart, Leah, currently make their home close to the high mountain trails and enjoy their blended family experience of ten children and two grandchildren. It has been his long-term dream to put into writing and have published several works that have been kicking around in his mind and on paper for many years. He looks forward to this next phase of life's wonderful adventures.